READ WELL®

Dinosaurs Before Dark

Teacher's Guide

Unit 12

au

au says /au/
Voiced

gi

gi says /j/
Voiced

be–

as in before

Note: See New and Important Objectives on page 2 for a complete list of skills taught and reviewed.

Critical Foundations in Primary Reading

Marilyn Sprick, Ann Watanabe, Karen Akiyama-Paik, and Shelley V. Jones

Sopris West®
EDUCATIONAL SERVICES

A Cambium Learning® Company

BOSTON, MA • LONGMONT, CO

ISBN 13-digit: 978-1-60218-535-7
ISBN 10-digit: 1-60218-535-2

7 8 9 10 11   B&B   16 15 14 13 12
166959/6-12

Table of Contents
Unit 12
Dinosaurs Before Dark

Table of Contents

Table of Contents

End of the Unit

Letter Sounds and Combinations

Cumulative Review of *Read Well 1* Sounds and Combinations (Ss, Ee, ee, Mm, Aa, Dd, th, Nn, Tt, Ww, Ii, Th, Hh, Cc, Rr, ea, sh, Sh, Kk, -ck, oo, ar, wh, Wh, ĕ, -y as in fly, Ll, Oo, Bb, all, Gg, Ff, Uu, er, oo as in book, Yy, a schwa, Pp, ay, Vv, Qq, Jj, Xx, or, Zz, a_e, -y as in baby, i_e, ou, ow as in cow, ch, Ch, ai, igh, o_e, ir) and:

Unit 2	Unit 3			Unit 5	Unit 6
aw	**ew**	**ue**	**u_e**	**ow**	**ge**
/aw/	/o͞o/	/o͞o/	/o͞o/	/ō͞ō/	/j/
Paw	**Crew**	**Blue**	**Flute**	**Snow**	**Page**
Voiced	Voiced	Voiced	Bossy E Voiced	Voiced (Long)	Voiced

Unit 6	Unit 7		Unit 8		Unit 10
-dge	**ci**	**ce**	**kn**	**ph**	**oa**
/j/	/sss/	/sss/	/nnn/	/fff/	/ō͞ō/
Badge	**Circle**	**Center**	**Knee**	**Phone**	**Boat**
Voiced	Unvoiced	Unvoiced	Voiced	Unvoiced	Voiced (Long)

Unit 11		Unit 12		Unit 13
oi	**ea**	**gi**	**au**	**oy**
/oi/	/ĕĕĕ/	/j/	/au/	/oy/
Point	**Bread**	**Giraffe**	**Astronaut**	**Boy**
Voiced	Voiced (Short)	Voiced	Voiced	Voiced

Affixes (including morphographs—affixes taught with meaning) and Open Syllables

Cumulative Review of *Read Well 1* Affixes (-ed, -en, -es, -ing, -ly, -s, -y, -tion) and:

Unit 2	Unit 3		Unit 5		Unit 6
re-	**un-**	**ex-**	**o**	**-ful**	**bi-**
Means again	**Means not**		Open syllable	**Means full of**	**Means two**
as in <u>re</u>read	as in <u>un</u>happy	as in <u>ex</u>cited	/ō/	as in color<u>ful</u>	as in <u>bi</u>cycle
			as in <u>o</u>pen and m<u>o</u>ment		

Unit 7	Unit 8	Unit 11	Unit 12	Unit 13	
de-	**-able**	**i**	**be-**	**-ous**	**dis-**
		Open syllable			
		/ī/			
as in <u>de</u>tective	as in comfort<u>able</u>	as in s<u>i</u>lence and p<u>i</u>lot	as in <u>be</u>fore	as in enorm<u>ous</u>	as in <u>dis</u>cover

Unit 14		Unit 15		Unit 16	
-al	**-ible**	**-or**	**-ment**	**-ic**	**pre-**
		Means one who			**Means before**
as in anim<u>al</u>	as in flex<u>ible</u>	as in act<u>or</u>	as in apart<u>ment</u>	as in scientif<u>ic</u>	as in <u>pre</u>view

Unit 17		Unit 18		Unit 19	
-ity	**-sion**	**-ness**	**-less**	**in-**	**im-**
			Means without		**Means not**
as in activ<u>ity</u>	as in permis<u>sion</u>	as in fair<u>ness</u>	as in help<u>less</u>	as in <u>in</u>sert	as in <u>im</u>possible

Introduction
Dinosaurs Before Dark

Story Notes

Dinosaurs Before Dark: Jack and Annie get a close-up view of the late Cretaceous period when the Magic Tree House sends them back in time. This first book in the Magic Tree House series gives us another opportunity to hook kids on books with a popular children's author. Quotes from the children below are sentiments we hope your kids will share as they get acquainted with Mary Pope Osborne.

> *I wish I could keep all your books in a glass case with a golden key.*
> —Luke R.
> *Your books really make me dream.*
> —Kurt K.

> **CAUTION**
> **(Reminder)**
> Do not read the Read Aloud recommendations during small group instruction. Reserve this time for students to read.

Recommended Read Alouds

The *Read Well 2* suggested Read Alouds enhance small group instruction—providing opportunities to further build background knowledge and vocabulary.

The Big Dinosaur Dig by Esther Ripley
Nonfiction • Science
Follow a real-life expedition to the Sahara Desert to hunt for dinosaur fossils. The team discovers bones that belong to one of the largest dinosaurs to walk the Earth.

Read Well Connections
Students learn how Earth has changed over time—providing a nonfiction backdrop to the period of time depicted in *Dinosaurs Before Dark*.

NOTE FROM THE AUTHORS

> **MILESTONE**
> By the end of this unit, your children and you have reached a milestone! They will have mastered all of the basic letter/sound associations needed to confidently read almost any children's trade book that might capture their interest!
>
> **CONGRATULATIONS ALL AROUND!**

New and Important Objectives
A Research-Based Reading Program

Phonemic Awareness
Phonics
Fluency
Vocabulary
Comprehension

Phonological and Phonemic Awareness
Segmenting; Blending; Rhyming; Onset and Rime; Counting Syllables

Phonics

Cumulative Letter Sounds and Combinations
Review • Ss, Ee, ee, Mm, Aa, Dd, th, Nn, Tt, Ww, Ii, Th, Hh, Cc, Rr, ea, sh, Sh, Kk, -ck, oo, ar, wh, Wh, ĕ, -y (as in fly), Ll, Oo, Bb, all, Gg, Ff, Uu, er, oo (as in book), Yy, a (schwa), Pp, ay, Vv, Qq, Jj, Xx, or, Zz, a_e, -y (as in baby), i_e, ou, ow (as in cow), ch, Ch, ai, igh, o_e, ir, aw, ew, ue, u_e, ow (as in snow), ge, -dge, ci, ce, kn, ph, oa, oi, ea (as in bread)

Cumulative Affixes, Morphographs, and Open Syllables
Review • -ed, -en, -er, -es, -est, -ing, -ly, -s, -y, -tion, re-, un-, ex-, o, -ful, bi-, de-, -able, i

★ New Letter Sounds, Combinations, Affixes, and Morphographs
au (as in astronaut) • Anatosaurus, Anatosauruses, astronaut, caught, caution, cautious, cautiously, exhaust, fault, haul, laundry, Paul, vault

gi (as in giraffe) • engine, gigantic, ginger, gingerbread, giraffe, magic, origin

be- (taught explicitly with review words)

★ New Proper Nouns
Annie, Pennsylvania, Pteranodon, Pteranodon's, Triceratops

★ New Contractions
he'll, they'd

★ New Pattern Words
barged, beast, bolted, bow, bowed, breath, bye, chart, chomping, clasp, clasped, curved, eased, feast, ferns, gasp, gasped, glance, glanced, gleaming, grip, gripped, grunt, grunted, hide, hole, horn, horns, huh, hunch, hunched, jeans, knelt, leaf, lips, lope, loped, nuts, oak, oops, peer, peered, peering, plus, porch, race, sail, sailed, scoop, scooped, shiny, shrug, shrugged, shut, slant, slanted, slapped, slope, sloping, slung, soar, soared, soaring, spun, stroke, tease, teasing, tilt, tilted, woods, yay

---

＊**Known Pattern Words With Affixes, Known Tricky Words With Affixes,** and **Known Multisyllabic Words With Affixes** have base words students have previously read. The words are new in this unit because they have not been previously read with the affix.

★ = New in this unit

Phonics (continued)

*Known Pattern Words With Affixes • beating, boldly, bony, cheerfully, closing, coasted, crawling, crouching, dazed, feels, flapping, flashing, flipped, fuzzy, glided, gliding, golden, grazing, groaned, heading, highest, hopped, hunted, kneeled, knives, leaped, longest, lying, minding, mouthful, nests, nudged, owns, pages, panting, paying, picking, pointing, poked, raced, rebuilt, recharged, restarted, riding, running, saving, screamed, sides, slammed, smelled, spending, spinning, squeezed, stepped, stuffed, swinging, tightly, topped, trying, tucked, wīnd, wīnding, wished

★New Compound and Hyphenated Words

baby-sat, backpack, bat-like, bookmark, bookmarks, duck-billed, hilltop, notebook, overhead, shield-like, spacecraft, treetops

★Other New Multisyllabic Words

afraid, alert, alive, aside, attention, bellow, bellowing, caption, cookie, crazy, dangling, distant, dizzy, elementary, engrave, engraved, engraving, examine, examined, glittering, heavy, horrible, ignore, ignored, incredibly, instead, monster, monster's, mutant, pencil, pocket, pretending, reptile, reptiles, rhinoceros, shadow, stammered, stampede, steadied, steady, supposed, teeny, teeter, teetered, tingle, trembled, tuba, ugly, valley, whistling, wobbly

*Known Multisyllabic Words With Affixes • castles, circled, forgetful, forgettable, towering, tumbled, unopened, unscrambled, wandering

★New Tricky Words

against, bush, bushes, heart, magnolia, medallion, miracle, scissors, shoulder, shriek, steak, waddled, weird, yeah

*Known Tricky Words With Affixes • climbing, covers, laughable, livable, shoulders, thoughtful, watchable

Fluency

Accuracy, Expression, Phrasing, Rate

Vocabulary

New • absolutely, bellow, bellowing, caption, cautiously, clasp, creature, crest, engraved, engraving, examine, medallion, miracle, mutant, panic, pant, peer, pretend, reptile, stampede, suspense, teeter, vanish

Review • adventure, amazing, ancient, colony, curious, dinosaur, extinct, graze, herbivore, hesitate, imagine, popular, protect, survive

Reviewed in Context • amazed, amazing, ancient, colony, contented, crouch, curious, dinosaur, frantic, graze, imagination, imagine, impressed, luscious, permission, plain, protect, shrug, wildlife

Idioms and Expressions

New • couldn't help himself, going too far, start after, stick close to, caught my eye, steady yourself

Comprehension

Unit Genres
Fiction • Imaginative
Nonfiction • Expository

Comprehension Processes
Build Knowledge: Factual, Procedural, Conceptual

Day	1	2	3	4	5	6	7	8	9	10
Remember										
Defining										
Identifying (recalling)	S,C	S,C	S,C	S	S,C	S,C	S	S,C	S,C	S,C
Using	S	S	S			S				S
Understand										
Defining (in your own words)		S,C	S						S	
Describing		S,C	S	S,C	C	S	S	S	S,C	
Explaining (rephrasing)	S,C	S	S	S,C	S	S	S		S	S
Illustrating										
Sequencing	C		S							
Summarizing		C			S	S				
Using	S	S,C	S,C	S,C	C	S,C	S	S,C	S,C	C
Visualizing		C					S		C	
Apply										
Demonstrating	S				S				S	
Explaining (unstated)	S	S,C	S	S	S,C	S,C	S,C	S,C	S	S,C
Illustrating	C	C							C	
Inferring	S	S	S	S	S	S	S,C	S,C	S	S,C
Making Connections (relating)	S	C				C				
Predicting	S		S,C				S,C	S	S	S
Using	S	S,C	S	S,C	S	S	S,C	S,C	S	
Analyze										
Classifying										
Comparing/Contrasting	S		C							
Distinguishing Cause/Effect										
Drawing Conclusions			C							
Inferring										
Evaluate										
Making Judgments										
Responding (personal)	C	C	C	C	C	C		C		S,C
Create										
Generating Ideas	C	C	C	C		C	C	C	C	

E = Exercise, S = Storybook, C = Comprehension & Skill

Comprehension (continued)

Skills and Strategies

Day	1	2	3	4	5	6	7	8	9	10
Priming Background Knowledge										
Setting a Purpose for Reading	S	S	S	S	S	S	S	S	S	S
Answering Questions	S	S,C	S	S	S	S	S,C	S	S	S
Asking Questions		S	S							
Visualizing		C					S		C	
Comprehension Monitoring/Fix Ups										
Does it Make Sense?		C	C	C	C	C	C	C	C	
Looking Back										
Restating										
Summarizing										
Main Idea							C			
Retelling										
Supporting Details							C			
Understanding Text Structure										
Title, Author, Illustrator	S,C	S	S		S		S		S	S
Fact or Fiction										
Genre (Classifying)										
Narrative										
Setting	S,C	C								
Main Character/Traits (Characterization)	S,C			S,C						C
Goal										
Problem/Solution							S	S		
Action/Events/Sequence	C		C	S				C		C
Outcome/Conclusion										
Lesson/Author's Message										
Expository										
Subject/Topic							C			
Heading										
Supporting Details (Facts/Information)					C		C			
Main Idea							C			
Using Graphic Organizers										
Chart										
Diagram (labeling)				C						
Hierarchy (topic/detail)							C			
K-W-L										
Map (locating, labeling)										
Matrix (compare/contrast)			C							
Sequence (linear, cycle, cause and effect)	C									
Story Map										
Web	C			C	C					

E = Exercise, S = Storybook, C = Comprehension & Skill

Comprehension (continued)

Study Skills

Day	1	2	3	4	5	6	7	8	9	10
Alphabetical Order										
Following Directions				C	C					
Locating Information	C	C		C	C					
Note Taking				C	C					
Previewing										
Reviewing		S	S	S	S	S	S	S	S	S
Test Taking								C	C	C
Using Glossary										
Using Table of Contents	S									
Viewing	S								S	
Verifying										

Writing in Response to Reading

Day	1	2	3	4	5	6	7	8	9	10
Sentence Completion	C	C	C	C	C	C	C	C	C	C
Making Lists										
Sentence Writing	C	C			C					C
Story Retell/Summary										
Fact Summary										
Paragraph Writing	C	C	C	C	C			C		
Report Writing										
Open-Ended Response		C	C			C	C	C		
Creative Writing		C							C	

Writing Traits

(Addressed within the context of Writing in Response to Reading)

Day	1	2	3	4	5	6	7	8	9	10
Ideas and Content										
Elaborating/Generating	C	C	C	C	C	C	C	C	C	
Organization										
Introduction										
Topic Sentence										
Supporting Details										
Sequencing	C						C			
Word Choice										
Sophisticated Words (Tier 2 and 3)	C	C	C	C	C	C	C	C	C	C
Conventions										
Capital	C	C	C	C	C	C	C	C	C	C
Ending Punctuation	C	C	C	C	C	C	C	C	C	C
Other (commas, quotation marks)					C					
Presentation										
Handwriting	C	C	C	C	C	C	C	C	C	C
Neatness	C	C	C	C	C	C	C	C	C	C

E = Exercise, S = Storybook, C = Comprehension & Skill

Daily Lesson Planning

LESSON PLAN FORMAT

Teacher-Directed 45 Minutes		Independent Teacher-Directed, as needed
Lesson Part 1 (Phonological Awareness, Phonics, Fluency, Comprehension) 15–20 Minutes	**Lesson Part 2** (Vocabulary, Fluency, Comprehension) 20–25 Minutes	**Lesson Part 3** (Vocabulary, Fluency, Comprehension) 15–20 Minutes
• Exercises	• Unit and/or Story Opener • Vocabulary • Interactive Story Reading • Short Passage Practice Timed Readings	• Story Reading With Partner or Whisper Reading • Comprehension and Skill Activities

HOMEWORK

Read Well Homework (blackline masters of new *Read Well 2* passages) provides an opportunity for children to celebrate accomplishments with parents. Homework should be sent home on routine days.

ORAL READING FLUENCY ASSESSMENT

Upon completion of this unit, assess each student and proceed to Unit 13, as appropriate.

WRITTEN ASSESSMENT

During the time students would normally complete Comprehension and Skill Activities, students will be administered a Written Assessment that can be found on page 75 in the students' *Activity Book 2*.

Note: See Making Decisions for additional assessment information.

DIFFERENTIATED LESSON PLANS

The differentiated lesson plans illustrate how to use materials for students with various learning needs. As you set up your unit plan, always include *Read Well 2* Exercises and Story Reading on a daily basis. Unit 12 includes 10-, 11-, 12-, and 13-Day Plans.

Plans	For groups that:
10-DAY	Complete Oral Reading Fluency Assessments with Passes and Strong Passes
11-, 12-, or 13-DAY	Have difficulty passing the unit Oral Reading Fluency Assessments

10-DAY PLAN

Day 1	Day 2	Day 3	Day 4	Day 5
Teacher-Directed • Exercise 1 • Unit and Story Opener: Dinosaurs Before Dark • Vocabulary, Ch. 1, 2 • Dinosaurs Before Dark, Ch. 1 (pages 1, 2) • Guide practice, as needed, on Book Journal Entry 1 and Comp & Skill 1 **Independent Work** • On Your Own: Partner or Whisper Read Dinosaurs Before Dark, Ch. 1 (pages 3–5) • Book Journal Entry 1 and Comp & Skill 1 **Homework** • Homework Passage 1	**Teacher-Directed** • Exercise 2 • Dinosaurs Before Dark, Ch. 2 (pages 6–8) • Guide practice, as needed, on Book Journal Entry 2 and Comp & Skill 2 **Independent Work** • On Your Own: Partner or Whisper Read, Dinosaurs Before Dark, Ch. 2 (pages 9–12) • Book Journal Entry 2 and Comp & Skill 2 **Homework** • Homework Passage 2	**Teacher-Directed** • Exercise 3 • Vocabulary, Ch. 3, 4 • Dinosaurs Before Dark, Ch. 3 (pages 13, 14) • Guide practice, as needed, on Book Journal Entry 3 and Comp & Skill 3 **Independent Work** • On Your Own: Partner or Whisper Read, Dinosaurs Before Dark, Ch. 3 (pages 15–17) • Book Journal Entry 3 and Comp & Skill 3 **Homework** • Homework Passage 3	**Teacher-Directed** • Exercise 4 • Dinosaurs Before Dark, Ch. 4 (pages 18–21) • Guide practice, as needed, on Book Journal Entry 4 and Comp & Skill 4 **Independent Work** • On Your Own: Partner or Whisper Read, Dinosaurs Before Dark, Ch. 4 (pages 22, 23) • Book Journal Entry 4 and Comp & Skill 4 **Homework** • Homework Passage 4	**Teacher-Directed** • Exercise 5 • Vocabulary, Ch. 5, 6 • Dinosaurs Before Dark, Ch. 5 (pages 24–26) • Guide practice, as needed, on Book Journal Entry 5 and Comp & Skill 5 **Independent Work** • On Your Own: Partner or Whisper Read, Dinosaurs Before Dark, Ch. 5 (pages 27–32) • Book Journal Entry 5 and Comp & Skill 5 • Optional Oral Reading Fluency Assessment* **Homework** • Homework Passage 5

* Unit 12 includes an optional mid-unit Oral Reading Fluency Assessment that can be administered individually by the teacher while students are working on their Book Journal and Comprehension and Skill activities.

10-DAY PLAN (continued)

Day 6	Day 7	Day 8	Day 9	Day 10
Teacher-Directed • Exercise 6 • Dinosaurs Before Dark, Ch. 6 (pages 33–37) • Guide practice, as needed, on Book Journal Entry 6 and Comp & Skill 6, 7 **Independent Work** • On Your Own: Partner or Whisper Read, Dinosaurs Before Dark, Ch. 6 (pages 38–42) • Book Journal Entry 6 and Comp & Skill 6, 7 **Homework** • Homework Passage 6	**Teacher-Directed** • Exercise 7 • Vocabulary, Ch. 7, 8 • Dinosaurs Before Dark, Ch. 7 (pages 43–45) • Guide practice, as needed, on Book Journal Entry 7 and Comp & Skill 8 **Independent Work** • On Your Own: Partner or Whisper Read, Dinosaurs Before Dark, Ch. 7 (pages 46, 47) • Book Journal Entry 7 and Comp & Skill 8 **Homework** • Homework Passage 7	**Teacher-Directed** • Exercise 8 • Dinosaurs Before Dark, Ch. 8 (pages 48, 49) • Guide practice, as needed, on Book Journal Entry 8 and Comp & Skill 9 **Independent Work** • On Your Own: Partner or Whisper Read, Dinosaurs Before Dark, Ch. 8 (pages 50–53) • Book Journal Entry 8 and Comp & Skill 9 **Homework** • Homework Passage 8	**Teacher-Directed** • Exercise 9 • Vocabulary, Ch. 9, 10 • Dinosaurs Before Dark, Ch. 9 (pages 54–57) • Guide practice, as needed, on Book Journal Entry 9 and Comp & Skill 10 **Independent Work** • On Your Own: Partner or Whisper Read, Dinosaurs Before Dark, Ch. 9 (pages 58–60) • Book Journal Entry 9 and Comp & Skill 10 **Homework** • Homework Passage 9	**Teacher-Directed** • Exercise 10 • Dinosaurs Before Dark, Ch. 10 (pages 61–64) • Guide practice, as needed, on Book Journal Entry 10 **Independent Work** • On Your Own: Partner or Whisper Read, Dinosaurs Before Dark, Ch. 10 (pages 65–68) • Book Journal Entry 10 • Written Assessment • Oral Reading Fluency Assessment* **Homework** • Homework Passage 10

11-, 12-, or 13-DAY PLAN • *Intervention*
For Days 1–10, follow 10-Day plan. Add Days 11, 12, 13 as follows:

Day 11 Extra Practice 1	Day 12 Extra Practice 2	Day 13 Extra Practice 3
Teacher-Directed • Decoding Practice • Fluency Passage **Independent Work** • Activity and Word Fluency A **Homework** • Fluency Passage	**Teacher-Directed** • Decoding Practice • Fluency Passage **Independent Work** • Activity and Word Fluency B **Homework** • Fluency Passage	**Teacher-Directed** • Decoding Practice • Fluency Passage **Independent Work** • Activity and Word Fluency A or B • Oral Reading Fluency Assessment* **Homework** • Fluency Passage

* The end-of-the-unit Oral Reading Fluency Assessments are individually administered by the teacher while students are working on their Written Assessments.

Materials and Materials Preparation

Core Lessons

Teacher Materials

READ WELL 2 MATERIALS

- Unit 12 Teacher's Guide
- Sound Cards
- Unit 12 Oral Reading Fluency Assessments foundon pages 138 and 139
- Group Assessment Record found in the *Assessment Manual*

SCHOOL SUPPLIES

Stopwatch or watch with a second hand

Student Materials

READ WELL 2 MATERIALS (for each student)

- *Dinosaurs Before Dark*
- *Exercise Book 2*
- *Activity Book 2* or copies of Unit 12 Comprehension and Skill Work and Book Journal
- Unit 12 Written Assessment found in *Activity Book 2*, page 75, and on the blackline master CD
- Unit 12 Certificate of Achievement/Goal Setting (BLM pages 140 and 141)
- Unit 12 Homework (blackline masters)
  See *Getting Started* for suggested homework routines.

SCHOOL SUPPLIES

Pencils, colors (optional—markers, crayons, or colored pencils)

> Make one copy per student of each blackline master, as appropriate for the group.
>
> *Note:* For new or difficult Comprehension and Skill Activities, make overhead transparencies from the blackline masters. Use the transparencies to demonstrate and guide practice.

> **BOOK JOURNAL**
> If students are using *Activity Book 2*, you will need to tear out the Book Journal (pages 43–48) and staple it together.

Extra Practice Lessons

> **CAUTION**
> Use these lessons only if needed. Students who need Extra Practice may benefit from one, two, or three lessons.

> **OPTIONAL MID-UNIT ASSESSMENT**
> Unit 12 includes an optional mid-unit assessment in addition to the end-of-unit Oral Reading Fluency Assessment.

Student Materials

READ WELL 2 MATERIALS (for each student, as needed)

See Extra Practice blackline masters located on the CD.

- Unit 12 Extra Practice 1: Decoding Practice, Fluency Passage, Word Fluency A, and Activity
- Unit 12 Extra Practice 2: Decoding Practice, Fluency Passage, Word Fluency B, and Activity
- Unit 12 Extra Practice 3: Decoding Practice, Fluency Passage, Word Fluency A or B, and Activity

SCHOOL SUPPLIES

Pencils, colors (markers, crayons, or colored pencils), highlighters

Important Tips

Independent Readers

When students reach the end of this unit, they will have mastered all of the basic letter/sound combinations and be able to read scores of multisyllabic words. They will also have learned 199 of the top 200 and 394 of the top 400 high-frequency words on Fry's word list.

Now is the time to actively encourage your students to read independently beyond the *Read Well 2* story selections. The Magic Tree House series is a treasure trove of books on topics young readers love. Annie and Jack visit a variety of historical settings, so students will be sure to find a period or topic that interests them. Here's a sampling:

The Knight at Dawn (Magic Tree House #2)
"Let's go back to the tree house right now," said Annie, "and find out if the magic person is a fact." Join Jack and Annie for another suspenseful journey into the past. Knights and castles, cobblestone streets, dungeons, and secret passageways make this second book in the Magic Tree House series an adventure kids won't want to miss.

Mummies in the Morning (Magic Tree House #3)
Jack and Annie travel to ancient Egypt, where they're surrounded by pyramids. The kids learn about false passages, tomb robbers, and real mummies! Along the way, they attempt to crack an ancient code.

Pirates Past Noon (Magic Tree House #4)
Jack and Annie find themselves staring at the blue sea in this adventure. Soon they see a ship flying a black flag emblazoned with a skull and crossbones, which can only mean one thing: pirates! When Jack and Annie encounter a black-toothed pirate named Cap'n Bones, a treasure map that promises gold, and a parrot named Polly, anything can happen!

Twister on Tuesday (Magic Tree House #23)
Jack and Annie travel back to the Kansas frontier of the late 1800s, where they learn all about prairie life. They attend a school with walls made of dirt and desks made from barrels. They write their assignments on tiny slates. They also encounter a giant twister!

Magic Treehouse Research Guides: For students who enjoy nonfiction, be sure to introduce the Magic Tree House Research Guides—nonfiction companions to the Magic Tree House adventures. Join Jack and Annie as they "find out the facts behind the fiction."

How to Teach the Lessons

Teach from this section. Each instructional component is outlined in an easy-to-teach format.

Exercise 1

- Unit and Story Opener: Dinosaurs Before Dark
- Vocabulary
- Story Reading 1
  With the Teacher: Chapter 1 (pages 1, 2)
  On Your Own: Chapter 1 (pages 3–5)
- Book Journal for Chapter 1
- Comprehension and Skill Activity 1

Exercise 2

- Story Reading 2
  With the Teacher: Chapter 2 (pages 6–8)
  On Your Own: Chapter 2 (pages 9–12)
- Book Journal for Chapter 2
- Comprehension and Skill Activity 2

Exercise 3

- Vocabulary
- Story Reading 3
  With the Teacher: Chapter 3 (pages 13, 14)
  On Your Own: Chapter 3 (pages 15–17)
- Book Journal for Chapter 3
- Comprehension and Skill Activity 3

Exercise 4

- Story Reading 4
  With the Teacher: Chapter 4 (pages 18–21)
  On Your Own: Chapter 4 (pages 22, 23)
- Book Journal for Chapter 4
- Comprehension and Skill Activity 4

Exercise 5

- Vocabulary
- Story Reading 5
  With the Teacher: Chapter 5 (pages 24–26)
  On Your Own: Chapter 5 (pages 27–32)
- Book Journal for Chapter 5
- Comprehension and Skill Activity 5

Note: Lessons include daily homework.

Exercise 6

- Story Reading 6
  With the Teacher: Chapter 6 (pages 33–37)
  On Your Own: Chapter 6 (pages 38–42)
- Book Journal for Chapter 6
- Comprehension and Skill Activities 6, 7

Exercise 7

- Vocabulary
- Story Reading 7
  With the Teacher: Chapter 7 (pages 43–45)
  On Your Own: Chapter 7 (pages 46, 47)
- Book Journal for Chapter 7
- Comprehension and Skill Activity 8

Exercise 8

- Story Reading 8
  With the Teacher: Chapter 8 (pages 48, 49)
  On Your Own: Chapter 8 (pages 50–53)
- Book Journal for Chapter 8
- Comprehension and Skill Activity 9

Exercise 9

- Vocabulary
- Story Reading 9
  With the Teacher: Chapter 9
  (pages 54–57)
  On Your Own: Chapter 9 (pages 58–60)
- Book Journal for Chapter 9
- Comprehension and Skill Activity 10

Exercise 10

- Vocabulary
- Story Reading 10
  With the Teacher: Chapter 10 (pages 61–64)
  On Your Own: Chapter 10 (pages 65–68)
- Book Journal for Chapter 10
- Written Assessment

Note: Lessons include daily homework.

❶ SOUND REVIEW

Use selected Sound Cards from Units 1–11.

PACING

Exercise 1 should take about 15 minutes.

★❷ NEW SOUND INTRODUCTION

- For Row A, tell students they will learn the sound for g-i. Say something like:
  Look at the picture. Say "g-i says /j/ as in giraffe." (g-i says /j/ as in giraffe)
  Read the sentence. (The giant gingerbread cookie looks like a giraffe.)
  Which three words have the /j/ sound? (giant, gingerbread, giraffe)

- For Row B, have students read the underlined sound, then the word.
- After reading the row, have students go back and read the whole words.

❸ SHIFTY WORD BLENDING

For each word, have students say the underlined sound. Then have them sound out the word smoothly and say it. Use the words in sentences, as appropriate.

❹ ACCURACY AND FLUENCY BUILDING

- For each task, have students say any underlined part, then read the word.
- Set a pace. Then have students read the whole words in each task and column.
- Provide repeated practice, building accuracy first, then fluency.

E1. Tricky Words

- For each Tricky Word, have students use the sounds and word parts they know to silently sound out the word. Use the word in a sentence to help with pronunciation.
- If the word is unfamiliar, tell students the word.

  yeah
  Look at the first word. Sound the word out silently. Thumbs up when you know the word. Use my sentence to help you pronounce the word. When my friend asked if I wanted to go to the park, I said . . . "*Yeah.*" Read the word three times. (yeah, yeah, yeah)

eight	The number after seven is . . . *eight.*
climbing	The squirrels are going up the tree. They are . . . *climbing* . . . the tree.
pushed	He pulled on the door when he should have . . . *pushed.*
sure	If you're not certain about something, you're not . . . *sure.*
minutes	One hour is equal to 60 . . . *minutes.*

- Have students go back and read the whole words in the column.

❺ MULTISYLLABIC WORDS

For each word in Rows A and B, have students read the syllables, then the whole word. Use the word in a sentence, as appropriate. For Row C, have students read the whole words.

monster	An imaginary creature is a . . . *monster.*
golden	The ring was shiny and bright. It was . . . *golden* . . . in color.
dinosaurs	Reptiles that lived millions of years ago were . . . *dinosaurs.*
disappeared	The magician put the rabbit in the hat. Then it . . . *disappeared.*
window	The room was hot, so Jay opened the . . . *window.*
pretend	Sammy likes to play make-believe. He likes to . . . *pretend.*
ladder	The firefighter climbed up the . . . *ladder.*
better	If you practice reading every day, you will get . . . *better.*

❻ MORPHOGRAPHS AND AFFIXES

- Have students read the underlined part, then the word.
- Repeat practice with whole words, mixing group and individual turns. Build accuracy, then fluency.

Dinosaurs Before Dark

Unit 12 Exercise 1
Use before Chapter 1

1. SOUND REVIEW Use selected Sound Cards from Units 1–11.

★ 2. NEW SOUND INTRODUCTION Introduce the new sound /j/ as in giraffe.

Ⓐ	**gi**	giraffe	The giant gingerbread cookie looks like a giraffe.

Ⓑ	register	imagine	giant	ginger	engine

3. SHIFTY WORD BLENDING For each word, have students say the underlined part, sound out smoothly, then read the word.

wings	sings	things	thinks	thanks

4. ACCURACY AND FLUENCY BUILDING For each column, have students say any underlined part, then read each word. Next, have students read the whole column.

A1 **Sound Practice**	B1 **Mixed Practice**	C1 **Bossy E**	D1 **Word Endings**	E1 **Tricky Words**
oak	know	sides	glasses	yeah
road	teeny	poked	tucked	eight
groaned	alone	rope	gripped	climbing
A2 **Names & Places**	woods	**C2** **Related Words**	whispered	pushed
Annie	moment	long	headed	sure
Frog Creek	sighed	longer	highest	minutes
Pennsylvania	pointing	longest	spending	
	shouted			

5. MULTISYLLABIC WORDS Have students read each word part, then read each whole word. For Row C, have students read each whole word.

Ⓐ	mon•ster	monster	gold•en	golden
Ⓑ	di•no•saurs	dinosaurs	dis•ap•peared	disappeared
Ⓒ	window	pretend	ladder	better

6. MORPHOGRAPHS AND AFFIXES Have students read the underlined part, then the word.

softly	watchable	helpful	until	between

33

TEAM EXPECTATIONS

Acknowledge Team Efforts

Pair your compliments with team expectations. Say something like: [Mona], I like the way you followed directions.

[Salim], you are sitting up so I can hear your great reading.

BUILD ACCURACY AND FLUENCY (Reminder)

For all rows and columns, follow the specific directions, then build accuracy and fluency with whole words.

COMPREHENSION PROCESSES
Remember, Understand, Apply

PROCEDURES

1. Introducing the Storybook

Identifying—Title, Author, Genre; Using Vocabulary—popular; Priming Background Knowledge; Inferring

Have students identify the title of their new storybook.
Say something like:
Everyone, look at the cover of the book.
What's the title of this book? (Dinosaurs Before Dark)

Who is the author? (Mary Pope Osborne)
Mary Pope Osborne is a *popular* author of children's books. Why do you think Mary Pope Osborne is a popular author? (People like her stories.)
This book is about dinosaurs.
You already know a lot about dinosaurs.
Partner 1s, tell Partner 2s an important fact about dinosaurs.
Partner 2s, tell Partner 1s an important fact about dinosaurs.
Let's list five important facts about dinosaurs on the board.
It will be fun to see if Mary Pope Osborne uses any of those facts in her story.

Do you think this book is fact or fiction? (fiction)
How can you tell? (The boy on the cover is riding on a dinosaur. There were no people in the time of the dinosaurs.)

2. Introducing the Table of Contents

Using the Table of Contents; Identifying—Titles; Inferring; Predicting
Turn to the Table of Contents. How many chapters are in this book? (10)
What's the name of the first chapter? (Into the Woods)
What page does it begin on? (It begins on page one.)

Sometimes the chapter titles give you clues about the story.
Where do you think this chapter is going to take place? (I think it will take place in the woods.)

What's the title of Chapter 2? (The Monster)
Chapter 2 may be exciting because it's about a monster.
Glance through the chapter titles. What else can you predict about the book?

Magic Tree House #1

Dinosaurs Before Dark

by Mary Pope Osborne

illustrated by Sal Murdocca

Random House

Contents

FOCUS ON SUSPENSE

After discussing the Table of Contents, say something like:
The first time I read this book I could hardly put it down.

At the end of every chapter, something happens. You want to keep reading because you are left wondering what will happen next. This is called *suspense*.

Mary Pope Osborne is great at creating suspense.

COMPREHENSION PROCESSES

Understand, Apply

PROCEDURES

Introducing Vocabulary

★pretend ★reptile ★creature ★crest ★absolutely ★couldn't help himself

- For each vocabulary word, have students read the word by parts, then read the whole word.
- Read the student-friendly explanations to students as they follow with their fingers. Then have students use the vocabulary word by following the gray text.
- Review and discuss the illustrations.
  Note: Student vocabulary pages for this unit are found in the students' *Exercise Book 2*.

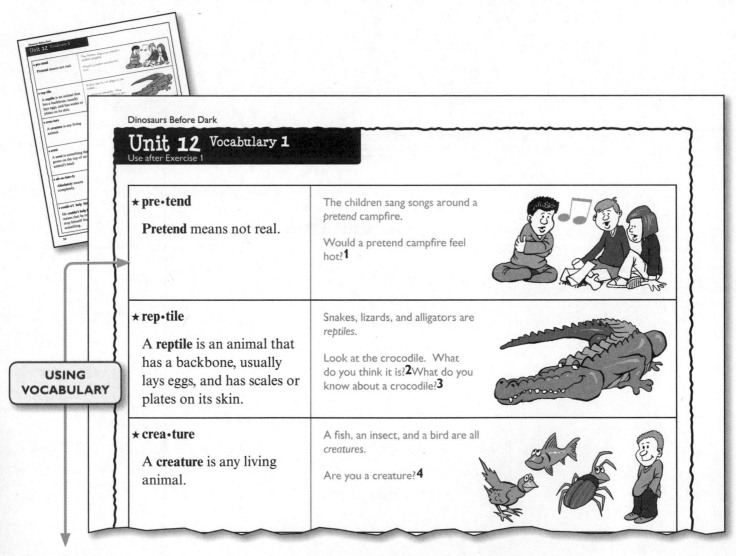

USING VOCABULARY

Dinosaurs Before Dark

Unit 12 Vocabulary 1
Use after Exercise 1

★ pre·tend **Pretend** means not real.	The children sang songs around a *pretend* campfire. Would a pretend campfire feel hot?**1**
★ rep·tile A **reptile** is an animal that has a backbone, usually lays eggs, and has scales or plates on its skin.	Snakes, lizards, and alligators are *reptiles*. Look at the crocodile. What do you think it is?**2** What do you know about a crocodile?**3**
★ crea·ture A **creature** is any living animal.	A fish, an insect, and a bird are all *creatures*. Are you a creature?**4**

❶ **Understand:** Using Vocabulary—pretend (No, a pretend campfire would not be hot.)

❷ **Apply:** Using Vocabulary—reptile (I think it's a reptile.)

❸ **Apply:** Using Vocabulary—reptile (It has a backbone. It probably lays eggs. It has scales or plates on its skin.)

❹ **Apply:** Making Connections, Using Vocabulary—creature (Yes, I'm a creature.)

★ = New in this unit

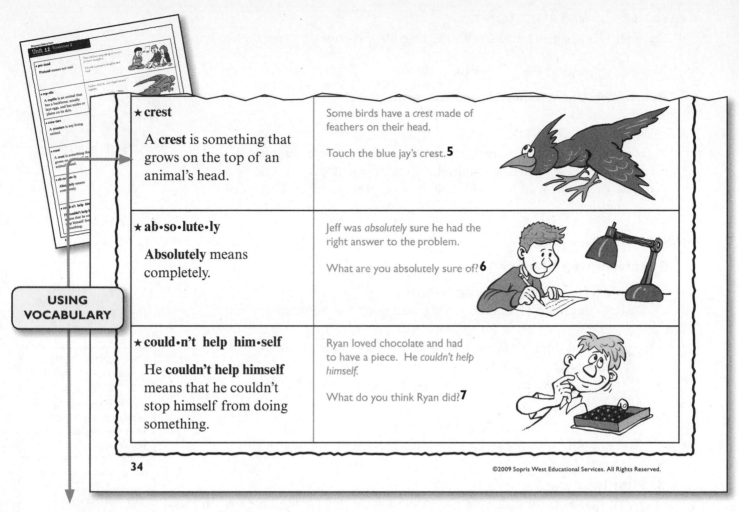

USING VOCABULARY

★ **crest** A **crest** is something that grows on the top of an animal's head.	Some birds have a *crest* made of feathers on their head. Touch the blue jay's crest. **5**	
★ **ab•so•lute•ly** **Absolutely** means completely.	Jeff was *absolutely* sure he had the right answer to the problem. What are you absolutely sure of? **6**	
★ **could•n't help him•self** He **couldn't help himself** means that he couldn't stop himself from doing something.	Ryan loved chocolate and had to have a piece. He *couldn't help himself.* What do you think Ryan did? **7**	

34

❺ **Apply:** Demonstrating; Using Vocabulary—crest

❻ **Apply:** Using Vocabulary—absolutely (I am absolutely sure I love to read.)

❼ **Apply:** Using Idioms and Expressions—couldn't help himself (Ryan ate some chocolate.)

USING VOCABULARY

Be enthusiastic about learning new words. Keep a running list of words you would like to use and encourage students to use. Keep the list handy when you are teaching. Put students' names on the board to acknowledge use of a word.
Say things like:
Wow! [Ray] used the word *pretend* when he talked about our new story.

CHAPTER 1 INSTRUCTIONS
Students read pages 1 and 2 with the teacher and pages 3–5 on their own.

COMPREHENSION PROCESSES
Remember, Understand, Apply, Analyze

COMPREHENSION BUILDING
- Encourage students to answer questions with complete sentences.
- If students have difficulty comprehending, think aloud with them, or reread the portion of the story that answers the question. Then repeat the question.

PROCEDURES

1. Introducing Chapter 1

Viewing; Identifying—Setting; Inferring
Discuss the main character, setting, and goal. Say something like:
Turn to page 1. Look at the picture. The main characters are Jack and Annie.
What are they doing? (They are walking in the woods. They are walking home.)
It looks to me like they're on their way home from school. Jack has his backpack.

The chapter title is "Into the Woods."
I wonder if they should go into the woods. What do you think?

2. First Reading
- Ask questions and discuss the story as indicated by the blue text in this teacher's guide.
- Mix group and individual turns, independent of your voice.
  Have students work toward a group accuracy goal of 0–2 errors.
  Quietly keep track of errors made by all students in the group.
- After reading the story, practice any difficult words.
  Reread the story if students have not reached the accuracy goal.

3. Second Reading, Short Passage Practice: Developing Prosody
- Demonstrate expressive, fluent reading of the first paragraph.
  Read at a rate slightly faster than the students' rate.
- Guide practice with your voice.
- Provide individual turns while others track with their fingers and whisper read.
- Repeat with one to three paragraphs at a time.
- Repeat steps with each remaining paragraph.

> **CORRECTING DECODING ERRORS**
>
> During story reading, gently correct any error, then have students reread the sentence.

> **REPEATED READINGS**
> **Prosody**
>
> On the second reading, students practice developing prosody—phrasing and expression. Research has shown that prosody is related to both fluency and comprehension.

1
Into the Woods

"Help! A monster!" said Annie.

"Yeah, sure," said Jack. "A real monster in Frog Creek, Pennsylvania."

"Run, Jack!" said Annie. She ran up the road.

Oh, brother.

This is what he got for spending time with his seven-year-old sister.

Annie loved pretend stuff. But Jack was eight and a half. He liked *real* things.

"Watch out, Jack! The monster's coming! Race you!"

1

After Reading Page 1

❶ **Analyze:** Contrasting—Main Characters; **Apply:** Using Vocabulary—pretend
How are Jack and Annie different from one another?
(Jack is eight and a half. Annie is seven. Jack likes real things. Annie likes pretend stuff.)

❷ **Remember:** Identifying—What
What did Annie say at the bottom of page 1?
(Watch out, Jack! The monster's coming! Race you!)

❸ **Understand:** Explaining; Using Vocabulary—pretend
Why did Annie say that?
(She was pretending there was a monster. She was playing.)

"No, thanks," said Jack.

Annie raced alone into the woods.

Jack looked at the sky. The sun was about to set.

"Come on, Annie! It's time to go home!"

But Annie had disappeared.

Jack waited.

No Annie.

"Annie!" he shouted again.

"Jack! Jack! Come here!"

Jack groaned. "This better be good," he said.

Jack left the road and headed into the woods. The trees were lit with a golden late-afternoon light.

"Come here!" called Annie.

There she was. Standing under a tall oak tree. "Look," she said. She was pointing at a rope ladder.

2

After Reading Page 2

❶ Apply: Inferring; Explaining
Why did Jack say, "It's time to go home"?
(It was getting dark. The book says, "The sun was about to set.")

❷ Remember: Identifying—Where
Where did Annie go?
(She went into the woods.)

❸ Understand: Explaining
In the middle of the page, Jack groaned and said, "This better be good." What did he mean?
(He meant that Annie had better have a good reason for running off.)

❹ Apply: Inferring
What do you think Annie found?
(a secret hiding place, a tree fort . . .)

CHAPTER 1 INSTRUCTIONS

Students read pages 3–5 without the teacher, independently or with partners.

COMPREHENSION PROCESSES

Understand, Apply

PROCEDURES FOR READING ON YOUR OWN

1. **Getting Ready**

   Have students turn to page 3.

2. **Setting a Purpose**

   Identifying—What; Inferring; Explaining; Using Vocabulary—hesitate

   Before students begin reading, say something like:

   On your own, read to the end of Chapter 1.

   Read to find out the answers to these questions:

   • What did Annie find?

   • Why did Jack hesitate before following Annie?

   • What made Jack change his mind and follow Annie?

   PREP NOTE
   Setting a Purpose
   Write questions on a chalkboard, white board, or large piece of paper before working with your small group.

3. **Reading on Your Own: Partner or Whisper Reading**

   • Have students take turns reading every other page with a partner or have students whisper read pages 3–5 on their own.

   • Continue having students track each word with their fingers.

   For Whisper Reading, say something like:

   Everyone, turn to page 3. This is where you're going to start reading on your own—without me. You will whisper read as you track with your finger so I can see where you are in your work.

   Turn to page 5. That's where you are going to stop reading.

   Now turn back to page 3.

   For Partner Reading, say something like:

   Everyone, turn to page 3. This is where you're going to start Partner Reading.

   Where are you going to sit? (at our desks, side by side)

   You will take turns reading pages. If you are the listener, what will you do? (keep my book flat, follow with my finger, compliment my partner)

   If you are the reader, what will you do? (keep my book flat, finger track, read quietly)

   Turn to page 5. That's where you are going to stop reading.

4. **Comprehension and Skill Work**

   Tell students they will start their Book Journal and do Comprehension and Skill Activity 1 after they read on their own. Guide practice, as needed. For teacher directions, see pages 26–28.

5. **Homework 1: New Passage**

The longest rope ladder Jack had ever seen.

"Wow," he whispered.

The ladder went all the way up to the top of the tree.

There—at the top—was a tree house. It was tucked between two branches.

"That must be the highest tree house in the world," said Annie.

"Who built it?" asked Jack. "I've never seen it before."

"I don't know. But I'm going up," said Annie.

"No. We don't know who it belongs to," said Jack.

"Just for a teeny minute," said Annie. She started up the ladder.

"Annie, come back!"

She kept climbing.

3

Jack sighed. "Annie, it's almost dark. We have to go home."

Annie disappeared inside the tree house.

"An-nie!"

Jack waited a moment. He was about to call again when Annie poked her head out of the tree house window.

"Books!" she shouted.

"What?"

"It's filled with books!"

Oh, man! Jack loved books.

He pushed his glasses into place. He gripped the sides of the rope ladder, and up he went.

COVER PAGE

COMPREHENSION PROCESSES
Remember, Understand

WRITING TRAITS
Conventions—Capital, Period
Presentation

Illustrating ⟶

Locating Information
Identifying—Title, Author, Illustrator

PROCEDURES
Discuss each step. Then have students complete the page independently.

1. Book Journal: Introduction
Explain that a book journal is a place to write down how we feel and what we think about the story. Say something like:
Read the title. (My Book Journal)
A book journal is made up of your personal thoughts and feelings about what the author has written.

After reading each chapter, you will have a chance to write something about what you just read. What you write in the journal is called an *entry*.

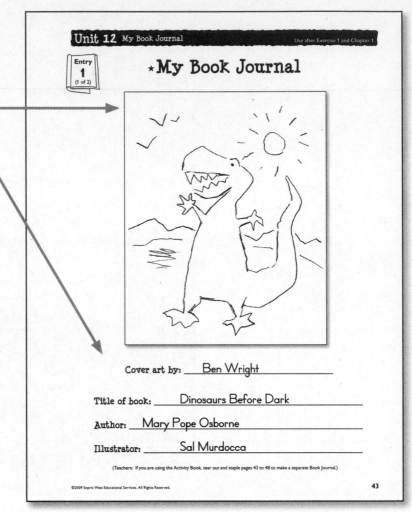

2. Cover: Locating and Filling In Information—Specific Instructions
• Have students identify what they will write on each line of the cover. Say something like:
Today, one of your jobs is to begin creating the cover.
Touch where you will write the title of the book. Remember, you'll need a capital at the beginning of each word, except for little words like *a* and *the* in the middle of the title.
Does this title have any little words? (no) Which words begin with a capital? (all the words)
Touch where you'll write the author's name.
How will you know how to spell Mary Pope Osborne's name? (Look at the book.)
In this book, you'll need to look at the title page for the illustrator's name.
Show me the title page. What's the illustrator's name? (Sal Murdocca)

• Have students illustrate a scene from the story after they've read more of the book.
What does the last line say? (cover art by . . .) That's right. The cover art is going to be by *you*.
Cover art is very important because its purpose is to get new readers interested in the book.
I'm going to have you read more of the book so you can decide what you want to draw.
For now, write your name after "Cover art by . . . "

ENTRY 1

COMPREHENSION PROCESSES

Remember, Understand, Apply, Create, Evaluate

WRITING TRAITS

Ideas and Content
Word Choice
Conventions—Complete Sentence, Capital, Period
Presentation

Responding

Using Graphic Organizer; Identifying— Main Character; Describing— Character Traits (Characterization)

Illustrating

Responding; Generating Ideas Explaining; Using Vocabulary—pretend

PROCEDURES

1. Characterization: Web, Illustrating—Specific Instructions (Items 1–3)

- Have students choose one of the main characters and write the character's name in the top blank.
- Have students write words or phrases that describe the character and then draw the character's picture.

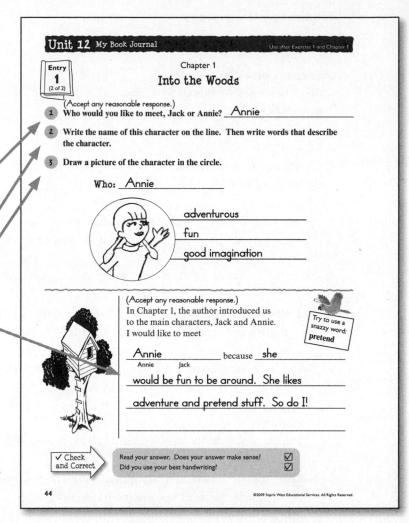

2. Characterization: Paragraph Writing—Specific Instructions

- Have students fill in the blank, then write a second sentence explaining what they like about the character they chose. Encourage students to use snazzy words.
- Think aloud with students and discuss possible answers, as needed. Say something like: After completing your web, you will complete your first entry.
  Read the sentences. (In Chapter 1, the author introduced us to the main characters . . .)
  Wouldn't that be fun to meet one of the characters? If you could invite Jack or Annie to visit us, who would you choose? Let's vote! Who would choose Annie? Who would choose Jack?

  There must be a reason that some of you chose Jack and some of you chose Annie. That's what you get to write about in your journal entry.

  Look at the sign that the bird is holding. Read it. (Try to use a snazzy word: pretend)
  What does *pretend* mean? (It means not real, or make-believe.) I could write "I would like to meet Jack because he knows the difference between real and *pretend*. He is older and more grown up than Annie."

STORY COMPREHENSION

COMPREHENSION PROCESSES
Remember, Understand

WRITING TRAITS
Organization—Sequencing
Conventions—Complete Sentence, Capital, Period
Presentation

PROCEDURES
For each step, demonstrate and guide practice, as needed. Then have students complete the page independently.

1. **Sentence Writing—Basic Instructions** (Item 1)
   Have students read the question and write a complete sentence, starting with "The main characters . . ."
   Remind students to start sentences with a capital and end with a period.

2. **Selection Response—Basic Instructions** (Item 2)
   Have students read the question and fill in the bubble for the correct answer.

3. **Sequence of Events: Chart, Sentence Completion—Basic Instructions** (Item 3)
   • Have students read the directions and sentence starters, then fill in the blanks to complete the sequence of events. Remind students to put a period at the end of each sentence.
   • Think aloud with students and discuss possible answers, as needed.

4. **Sequence of Events: Paragraph Writing—Specific Instructions** (Item 4)
   • Have students read the instructions and write a paragraph using the events from the graphic organizer. Say something like:
   After you complete the chart, you're going to use the chart to write a paragraph about what happened in Chapter 1. In most stories, the order in which things happen—first, next, and so on—is important.
   This is called the *sequence*.

   Read the sentence that will start your paragraph. (At the beginning of the chapter . . .)
   Look at the box with the heading. What does the heading say? (First Event)
   What happened first in the chapter? (Annie ran off into the woods.)
   When we write about the first event, we can begin . . . "At the beginning of the chapter . . . "
   Read and finish that sentence with me. At the beginning of the chapter, Annie ran off into the woods.

   In the next event, who followed Annie into the woods? (Jack)
   So after the word "next," what would you write? (Jack followed Annie into the woods.)

   • Repeat for the remainder of the events. Remind students to end sentences with a period.

**Identifying—
Main Characters**

Identifying—Setting

**Using Graphic
Organizer
Identifying—Events**

**Sequencing
Explaining—Events**

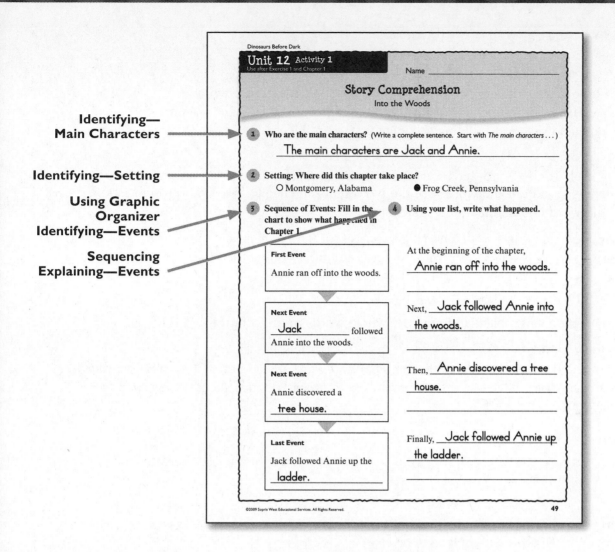

Dinosaurs Before Dark

Unit 12 Activity 1
Use after Exercise 1 and Chapter 1

Name _____

Story Comprehension
Into the Woods

1 Who are the main characters? (Write a complete sentence. Start with *The main characters . . .*)

The main characters are Jack and Annie.

2 Setting: Where did this chapter take place?

○ Montgomery, Alabama   ● Frog Creek, Pennsylvania

3 Sequence of Events: Fill in the chart to show what happened in Chapter 1

4 Using your list, write what happened.

First Event

Annie ran off into the woods.

At the beginning of the chapter, Annie ran off into the woods.

Next Event

Jack _____ followed Annie into the woods.

Next, Jack followed Annie into the woods.

Next Event

Annie discovered a tree house.

Then, Annie discovered a tree house.

Last Event

Jack followed Annie up the ladder.

Finally, Jack followed Annie up the ladder.

49

❶ SOUND REVIEW

❷ ACCURACY AND FLUENCY BUILDING
- For each task, have students say any underlined part, then read the word.
- Set a pace. Then have students read the whole words in each task and column.
- Provide repeated practice, building accuracy first, then fluency.

E1. Tricky Words
- For each Tricky Word, have students use the sounds and word parts they know to silently sound out the word. Use the word in a sentence to help with pronunciation.
- If the word is unfamiliar, tell students the word.

touched	Juan said that his rabbit's fur is soft. But I have never . . . *touched* . . . his rabbit.
hey	If you want to get someone's attention, you can say . . . *"Hey."*
covers	The little girl hid her head under the . . . *covers.*
enough	I'm full. I've had . . . *enough.*

- Have students go back and read the whole words in the column.

E2. Compound Words
- As needed, remind students that a compound word is made up of two small words.
- For each word, have students figure out the compound word silently, then read the word.

❸ MULTISYLLABIC WORDS
For each word, have students read the syllables, then the whole word. Use the word in a sentence, as appropriate.

reptile	A lizard is a . . . *reptile.*
elementary	We don't go to high school or middle school. We go to . . . *elementary* . . . school.
skinny	The opposite of fat is . . . *skinny.*
whistling	I could hear the wind . . . *whistling* . . . through the trees.
distance	The library was far away. It was a long . . . *distance* . . . to walk.
supposed	The new store did not open today, even though it was . . . *supposed* . . . to.

❹ MORPHOGRAPHS AND AFFIXES
- Have students read the underlined part, then the word.
- Review the morphographs *re-*, *un-*, and *-ful*, as time allows.
- Repeat practice with whole words, mixing group and individual turns.

❺ DINOSAUR WORDS
- Tell students they will be reading dinosaur names or words related to dinosaurs.
- Have students read each word, using the pronunciation guide for help.
- Use the word in a sentence, as needed.

❻ GENERALIZATION: READING NEW WORDS IN PARAGRAPHS
- Have students read the paragraph silently, then out loud. Tell students to use the sounds and word parts they know to read any difficult words.
- Repeat practice, as needed.

Dinosaurs Before Dark

Unit 12 Exercise 2
Use before Chapter 2

1. SOUND REVIEW Have students review sounds for accuracy, then for fluency.

Ⓐ	oa as in boat	ea as in bread	ge as in page	ew as in crew	gi as in giraffe
Ⓑ	kn	aw	ce	-dge	ci

2. ACCURACY AND FLUENCY BUILDING For each column, have students say any underlined part, then read each word. Next, have students read the whole column.

A1 New Sound Practice	**B1** Mixed Practice	**C1** Word Endings	**D1** Word Endings	**E1** Tricky Words
g<u>i</u>ant	cr<u>e</u>st	glide	<u>trying</u>	touched
en<u>gi</u>ne	s<u>i</u>lk	gliding	<u>pretending</u>	hey
or<u>i</u>g<u>i</u>n	sh<u>u</u>t	shine	<u>spinning</u>	covers
imag<u>i</u>ne	<u>ow</u>ns	shiny	<u>pointed</u>	enough
A2 Related Words	c<u>ur</u>ved	study	<u>slanted</u>	**E2** Compound Words
soar	pa<u>ge</u>	studied	<u>screamed</u>	backpack
soared	hole		<u>squeezed</u>	bookmark
soaring	b<u>ea</u>k		<u>glanced</u>	treetops
	shu<u>sh</u>			

3. MULTISYLLABIC WORDS Have students read each word part, then read each whole word.

Ⓐ	rep·tile	reptile	el·e·men·ta·ry	elementary
Ⓑ	skin·ny	skinny	whis·tling	whistling
Ⓒ	dis·tance	distance	sup·posed	supposed

4. MORPHOGRAPHS AND AFFIXES Have students read each underlined part, then the word.

dire<u>ction</u>	absolute<u>ly</u>	<u>re</u>turned	<u>un</u>opened	care<u>ful</u>

5. DINOSAUR WORDS Have students use the sounds and word parts they know and the pronunciation guide to read the word. Then have them read the sentence.

Pteranodon	Tuh-ran-uh-don	A <u>Pteranodon</u> is a flying dinosaur.

6. GENERALIZATION Have students read the paragraph silently, then out loud. (New words: porch, trembled, peering, weird)

Beth looked over at the neighbor's old castle from her front porch. Beth thought she saw a strange creature peering at her through the gate. She trembled. "It's okay," she told herself. "It's just my imagination." Even though she was scared, Beth walked straight past the weird house as she headed to school.

35

KEEP LESSONS MOVING WITH FINGER TRACKING

Always require finger tracking. This will:
• Prevent having to stop to help students find their places.
• Ensure students are practicing even when it's someone else's turn.
• Allow you to monitor on-task behavior.
• Increase focus and accuracy.

GENERALIZATION (Reminder)

The generalization task provides an opportunity for you to informally assess students' ability to read new words that have not been pretaught.

CHAPTER 2 INSTRUCTIONS
Students read pages 6–8 with the teacher and pages 9–12 on their own.

COMPREHENSION PROCESSES
Remember, Understand, Apply

PROCEDURES

1. Reviewing Chapter 1

Explaining; Using Vocabulary—hesitate

Review Chapter 1 by quickly discussing the questions from Setting a Purpose. Say something like:

You read the last part of Chapter 1 on your own. Let's see what you found out.

What did Annie find? (She found a tree house full of books.)

Why did Jack hesitate before following Annie? (He didn't think they should go up in the tree house. It didn't belong to them. He had never seen it before. It was really high . . .)

What made Jack change his mind and follow her up? (The tree house was full of books, and Jack loves books.)

2. Introducing Chapter 2

Identifying—Title; Inferring

What's the title of this chapter? (The title is "The Monster.")

Why do you think the chapter is called "The Monster"? (The kids are going to find a monster . . .)

3. First Reading

- Ask questions and discuss the story as indicated by the blue text in this teacher's guide.
- Mix group and individual turns, independent of your voice.
  Have students work toward a group accuracy goal of 0–4 errors.
  Quietly keep track of errors made by all students in the group.
- After reading the story, practice any difficult words. Reread the story if students have not reached the accuracy goal.

4. Second Reading, Timed Readings: Repeated Reading

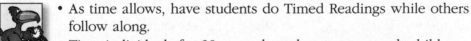

- As time allows, have students do Timed Readings while others follow along.
- Time individuals for 30 seconds and encourage each child to work for a personal best.
- Determine words correct per minute. Record student scores.

5. Partner or Whisper Reading: Repeated Reading

Before beginning independent work, have students finger track and partner or whisper read.

2

The Monster

Jack crawled through a hole in the tree house floor.

Wow. The tree house *was* filled with books. Books everywhere. Very old books with dusty covers. New books with shiny, bright covers.

"Look. You can see far, far away," said Annie. She was peering out the tree house window.

Jack looked out the window with her. Down below were the tops of the other trees. In the distance he saw the Frog Creek library.

6

The elementary school. The park.

Annie pointed in the other direction.

"There's our house," she said.

Sure enough. There was their white wooden house with the green porch. Next door was their neighbor's black dog, Henry. He looked very tiny.

"Hi, Henry!" shouted Annie.

"Shush!" said Jack. "We're not supposed to be up here."

He glanced around the tree house again.

"I wonder who owns all these books," he said. He noticed bookmarks were sticking out of many of them.

"I like this one," said Annie. She held up a book with a castle on the cover.

"Here's a book about Pennsylvania," said Jack. He turned to the page with the book-mark.

7

After Reading Page 7

❶ Understand: Describing
Describe what Jack and Annie could see from the tree house.
(They could see Frog Creek library, the school, the park, their house, and the neighbor's dog, Henry.)

❷ Remember: Identifying—Where
Jack picked up a book about Pennsylvania. Where do Jack and Annie live?
(They live in Frog Creek, Pennsylvania.)

Note: Have students look back to Chapter 1 if they can't remember where Jack and Annie live.

"Hey, there's a picture of Frog Creek in here," said Jack. "It's a picture of *these* woods!"

"Oh, here's a book for you," said Annie. She held up a book about dinosaurs. A blue silk bookmark was sticking out of it.

"Let me see it." Jack set down his backpack and grabbed the book from her.

"You look at that one, and I'll look at the one about castles," said Annie.

"No, we better not," said Jack. "We don't know who these books belong to."

But even as he said this, Jack opened the dinosaur book to where the bookmark was. He couldn't help himself.

He turned to a picture of an ancient flying reptile. A Pteranodon.

He touched the huge bat-like wings.

"Wow," whispered Jack. "I wish I could

8

After Reading Page 8
(Have students complete the sentence on page 9.)

❶ **Remember:** Identifying—What
Jack opened a book. What was it about?
(The book was about dinosaurs.)

❷ **Remember:** Identifying—What
What did Jack see in the book?
(He saw a Pteranodon.)

❸ **Apply:** Inferring; Explaining; Using Vocabulary—
ancient, reptile
Why was the Pteranodon called an *ancient* flying *reptile*?
(Pteranodons lived millions of years ago . . .)

❹ **Remember:** Identifying—What
What did Jack wish for?
(He wished he could see a real Pteranodon.)

CHAPTER 2 INSTRUCTIONS

Students read pages 9–12 without the teacher, independently or with partners.

COMPREHENSION PROCESSES

Remember, Apply

PROCEDURES

1. Getting Ready

Have students turn to page 9.

2. Setting a Purpose

Identifying—What; Asking Questions; Defining and Using Vocabulary—suspense

Before students begin reading, say something like:

As you read the next pages, try to answer these questions:

- What did Annie and Jack see from the tree house?
- What did the tree house do?
- What do you want to find out in Chapter 3?

When you finish Chapter 2, you will want to read Chapter 3. That's the sign of a great book.

Remember, Mary Pope Osborne usually ends a chapter making us wonder what will happen next. What's that called? (It's called suspense.)

What does suspense make you wonder about? (It makes me wonder what will happen next.)

When you finish Chapter 2, you'll have to put your book down so you can do your other work.

It will be fun for us to find out what happens next when we read together tomorrow.

3. Reading on Your Own: Partner or Whisper Reading

- Have students take turns reading every other page with a partner, or have students whisper read pages 9–12 on their own.
- Continue having students track each word with their fingers.

4. Comprehension and Skill Work

Tell students that they will work on their Book Journal and do Comprehension and Skill Activity 2 after they read on their own. Guide practice, as needed. For teacher directions, see pages 38 and 39.

5. Homework 2: New Passage

PREP NOTE

Setting a Purpose

Write questions on a chalkboard, white board, or large piece of paper before working with your small group.

see a Pteranodon for real."

Jack studied the picture of the odd-looking creature soaring through the sky.

"Ahhh!" screamed Annie.

"What?" said Jack.

"A monster!" Annie cried. She pointed to the tree house window.

"Stop pretending, Annie," said Jack.

"No, really!" said Annie.

Jack looked out the window.

A giant creature was gliding above the treetops! He had a long, weird crest on the back of his head. A skinny beak. And huge bat-like wings!

It was a real live Pteranodon!

The creature curved through the sky. He was coming straight toward the tree house. He looked like a glider plane!

The wind began to blow.

9

The leaves trembled.

Suddenly the creature soared up. High into the sky. Jack nearly fell out the window trying to see it.

10

The wind picked up. It was whistling now.
The tree house started to spin.
"What's happening?" cried Jack.
"Get down!" shouted Annie.

11

She pulled him back from the window.

The tree house was spinning. Faster and faster.

Jack squeezed his eyes shut. He held on to Annie.

Then everything was still.

Absolutely still.

Jack opened his eyes. Sunlight slanted through the window.

There was Annie. The books. His backpack.

The tree house was still high up in an oak tree.

But it wasn't the *same* oak tree.

12

ENTRY 2

COMPREHENSION PROCESSES

Apply, Create, Evaluate

WRITING TRAITS

Ideas and Content
Word Choice
Conventions—Complete Sentence,
Capital, Period
Presentation

Responding; Making Connections
Generating Ideas; Using Vocabulary—
creature, absolutely; Visualizing

PROCEDURES

For each step, demonstrate and guide practice, as needed. Then have students complete the page independently.

Personal Response: Creative Writing—Specific Instructions

Have students write a paragraph about how they would feel if they saw a dinosaur from their bedroom window. Encourage students to use snazzy vocabulary words in their writing. Remind them to start sentences with a capital and end with a period. Say something like:

Find Entry 2 in your Book Journal. Read the sentences. (In Chapter 2, Jack and Annie saw a dinosaur. Imagine seeing a dinosaur from your bedroom window. What would you say?)

This is going to be a fun entry. I'm going to look forward to reading your responses. Read the snazzy words. (creature, absolutely)

Remember, we're going to try to use those words in our journals.

The entry is started for us. This is what I might write: "Oh my! There is a huge creature outside my window. I can't believe my eyes. I'm absolutely sure it's a dinosaur! How could that be?"

Before you write, try to imagine or visualize actually seeing a dinosaur outside your window. Think about what you would say!

Self-monitoring

Have students check and correct their work.

STORY COMPREHENSION ★SUMMARIZING AND VOCABULARY ★SUSPENSE

COMPREHENSION PROCESSES
Remember, Understand

WRITING TRAITS
Conventions—Capital, Period
Locating Information, Summarizing

Identifying—What, Setting

Identifying—What

Identifying—Author, Genre; Defining and Using Vocabulary—suspense

Identifying—What

PROCEDURES
For each step, demonstrate and guide practice, as needed. Then have students complete the page independently.

★Summarizing: Sentence Completion—Basic Instructions (Items 1–3)
Have students read the paragraphs and fill in the blanks. Remind them to look back in their books for help.

Vocabulary ★ Suspense—Specific Instructions
Have students read the explanation of the vocabulary word "suspense."
Read the information below the title "Vocabulary ★Suspense." (The author is very good at . . .) After reading Chapters 1 and 2, did you wonder what was going to happen next? (yes) When an author makes the readers wonder about what will happen, that is creating suspense. Everyone, say that snazzy word *suspense*. (suspense)

1. **Answering Questions—Basic Instructions** (Item 1)
   Have students read the question and write the answer in the blank. Guide students to locate the information, if needed.

2. **Selection Response—Specific Instructions** (Item 2)
   • Have students read the sentences, then check the correct answers. Say something like: Read the instructions for Item 2. (Check two ways . . .) Now, read the first choice after I read the sentence starter. The author created suspense by making us wonder . . . (why Jack and Annie saw a live Pteranodon in Frog Creek.) Did you wonder why Jack and Annie saw a live Pteranodon in Frog Creek? (yes) Yes, that is one way the author created suspense. So place a check next to that choice.
   • Repeat for the remaining choices.

★ = New in this unit

Dinosaurs Before Dark

Unit 12 Activity 2
Use after Exercise 2 and Chapter 2

Name _____

Story Comprehension ★Summarizing
The Monster

1. At the beginning of the book, Jack and Annie discovered a tree house full of __books__. There was a book about Pennsylvania with a picture of Frog Creek. Jack and Annie lived in __Pennsylvania.__

Look in your storybook on pages 8 and 9.

2. At the beginning of Chapter 2, Jack opened a book about __dinosaurs.__ He turned to a picture of a Pteranodon. "Wow," whispered Jack. "I wish I could __see a Pteranodon for real.__"
Then a live Pteranodon appeared.

Look in your storybook on page 12.

3. At the end of Chapter 2, the tree house began __to spin.__ When Jack opened his eyes, everything was still. The tree house was still high up in an oak tree. But it wasn't the __same__ oak tree.

Vocabulary ★Suspense
The author is very good at creating suspense in her stories. Suspense is a feeling of excitement. It makes us curious. Suspense makes us wonder what is going to happen next.

1. Who is the author of this book? __Mary Pope Osborne__

2. Check two ways the author made us curious. She created suspense by making us wonder . . .
   ✓ why Jack and Annie saw a live Pteranodon in Frog Creek.
   __ where Jack and Annie went to school.
   ✓ why the tree house ended up in a different oak tree.

50

©2009 Sopris West Educational Services. All Rights Reserved.

❶ SOUND REVIEW

★❷ NEW SOUND INTRODUCTION
- Have students look at the picture. Tell students <u>a</u>-<u>u</u> says /au/ as in astronaut. Say something like:

  Look at the picture. Say "<u>a</u>-<u>u</u> says /au/ as in astronaut." (<u>a</u>-<u>u</u> says /au/ as in astronaut)

  Read the sentence. (Paul the astronaut will haul the flat rock back to the spacecraft.)

  Which three words have the /au/ sound? (Paul, astronaut, haul)

- For Row B, have students read the underlined sound, then the word.
- After reading the row, have students go back and read the whole words.

❸ ACCURACY AND FLUENCY BUILDING
- For each task, have students say any underlined part, then read the word.
- Set a pace. Then have students read the whole words in each task and column.
- Provide repeated practice, building accuracy first, then fluency.

C1. Reading by Analogy

Have students figure out how to say *-ind* by reading other words they know.

E1. Tricky Words
- For each Tricky Word, have students use the sounds and word parts they know to silently sound out the word. Use the word in a sentence to help with pronunciation.
- If the word is unfamiliar, tell students the word.

yeah	When I talk to my friends, instead of saying yes, I say . . . *yeah.*
covered	It snowed last night, so the streets are . . . *covered* . . . with snow.
millions	When the family won the contest, they won . . . *millions* . . . of dollars.
period	Dinosaurs lived during the Cretaceous . . . *period.*
either	My friends are not going to the party. I am not going . . . *either.*
ancient	Something that is really, really old is . . . *ancient.*

- Have students go back and read the whole words in the column.

❹ MULTISYLLABIC WORDS

For each word, have students read the syllables, then the whole word. Use the word in a sentence, as appropriate.

stammered	My teacher was surprised to see me at the store. "Hello," he . . . *stammered.*
vanished	The rabbit was suddenly gone. It . . . *vanished.*
volcanoes	Hawaii has lots of . . . *volcanoes.*
crazy	Jason really, really likes toys. He is . . . *crazy* . . . about toys.
supposed	The assembly is just for fifth grade students. We aren't . . . *supposed* . . . to go.
impossible	If something's not possible, it's . . . *impossible.*

❺ AFFIXES

★Have students practice reading *be-* and the related words. Use each word in a sentence.

⑥ **DINOSAUR WORDS**
- Have students read each word, using the pronunciation guide for help.
- Use the word in a sentence, as needed.

Dinosaurs Before Dark

Unit 12 Exercise 3
Use before Chapter 3

1. SOUND REVIEW Use selected Sound Cards from Units 1–12.

★2. NEW SOUND INTRODUCTION Introduce the new sound /au/ as in astronaut.

Ⓐ		
au	astron<u>au</u>t	P<u>au</u>l the astron<u>au</u>t will h<u>au</u>l the flat rock back to the spacecraft.

| Ⓑ | f<u>au</u>lt | l<u>au</u>ndry | h<u>au</u>l | <u>Au</u>gust | v<u>au</u>lt |

3. ACCURACY AND FLUENCY BUILDING For each column, have students say any underlined part, then read each word. Next, have students read the whole column.

A1 New Sound Practice	**B1** Mixed Practice	**C1** Reading by Analogy	**D1** Word Endings	**E1** Tricky Words
<u>gi</u>ant	spr<u>ea</u>d	find	<u>stepped</u>	yeah
ima<u>gi</u>ne	c<u>oa</u>sted	finding	<u>soaring</u>	covered
en<u>gi</u>ne	kept		<u>reptiles</u>	millions
A2 Morphographs & Affixes	j<u>oi</u>n	mind		period
<u>ex</u>actly	f<u>er</u>ns	minding	slope	either
<u>de</u>cide	<u>kn</u>ow		sloping	ancient
liv<u>able</u>	b<u>a</u>se	wind		
bold<u>ly</u>	n<u>u</u>ts	winding	glide	
	g<u>uar</u>d		glided	

4. MULTISYLLABIC WORDS Have students read each word part, then read each whole word.

Ⓐ	stam•mered	stammered	van•ished	vanished
Ⓑ	vol•ca•noes	volcanoes	cra•zy	crazy
Ⓒ	sup•posed	supposed	im•pos•si•ble	impossible

5. AFFIXES Have students practice reading "be-" and the related words.

| ★ be- | <u>be</u>cause | <u>be</u>gin | <u>be</u>fore | <u>be</u>come |

6. DINOSAUR WORDS Have students use the sounds and word parts they know and the pronunciation guide to read the words.

| Pteranodon | Tuh-ran-uh-don | Cretaceous | Cri-tay-shus |

> **BUILDING INDEPENDENCE (Reminder)**
>
> Some students will try to follow your voice instead of learning to read the sounds and words. Therefore, it is important for you to demonstrate and guide practice only as needed.
>
> Give students many opportunities to respond without your assistance—with groups and individuals. Encourage independence.

COMPREHENSION PROCESSES

Understand, Apply

PROCEDURES

Introducing Vocabulary

> ★vanish, ancient ★examine ★cautiously ★mutant ★going too far

- For each vocabulary word, have students read the word by parts, then read the whole word.
- Read the student-friendly explanations to students as they follow with their fingers. Then have students use the vocabulary word by following the gray text.
- Review and discuss the illustrations.
  Note: Student vocabulary pages for this unit are found in the students' *Exercise Book 2*.

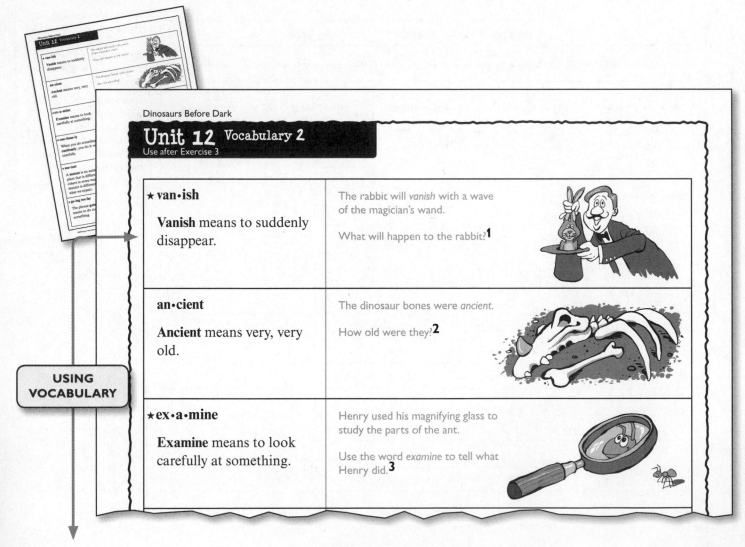

USING VOCABULARY

Dinosaurs Before Dark

Unit 12 Vocabulary 2
Use after Exercise 3

★ van•ish **Vanish** means to suddenly disappear.	The rabbit will *vanish* with a wave of the magician's wand. What will happen to the rabbit?**1**
an•cient **Ancient** means very, very old.	The dinosaur bones were *ancient*. How old were they?**2**
★ex•a•mine **Examine** means to look carefully at something.	Henry used his magnifying glass to study the parts of the ant. Use the word *examine* to tell what Henry did.**3**

❶ **Understand:** Using Vocabulary—vanish (It will disappear. It will vanish.)

❷ **Apply:** Using Vocabulary—ancient (The bones were millions of years old.)

❸ **Apply:** Using Vocabulary—examine (He examined the ant.)

★ = New in this unit

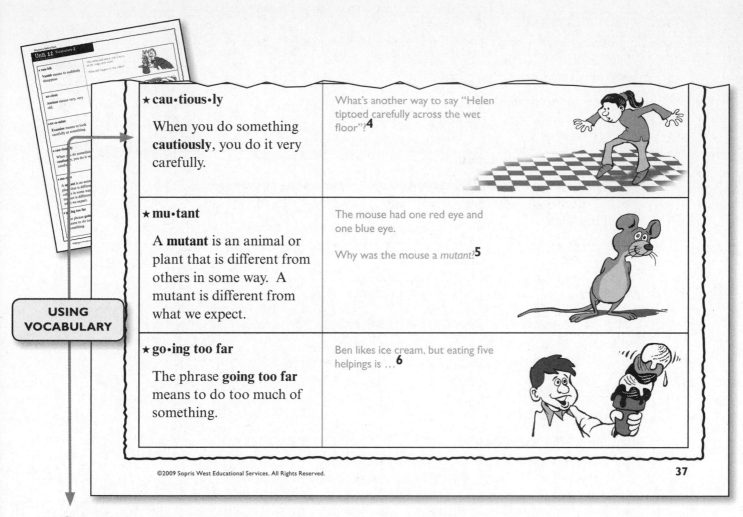

USING VOCABULARY

★ **cau·tious·ly**

When you do something **cautiously**, you do it very carefully.

What's another way to say "Helen tiptoed carefully across the wet floor"?**4**

★ **mu·tant**

A **mutant** is an animal or plant that is different from others in some way. A mutant is different from what we expect.

The mouse had one red eye and one blue eye.

Why was the mouse a *mutant*?**5**

★ **go·ing too far**

The phrase **going too far** means to do too much of something.

Ben likes ice cream, but eating five helpings is … **6**

37

❹ **Apply:** Using Vocabulary—cautiously (Helen tiptoed cautiously across the wet floor.)

❺ **Apply:** Defining and Using Vocabulary—mutant (The mouse was a mutant because it had one red eye and one blue. Different-colored eyes is not what we expect.)

❻ **Apply:** Using Idioms and Expressions—going too far (going too far)

USING VOCABULARY

Be enthusiastic about learning new words. Keep a running list of words you would like to use and encourage students to use. Keep the list handy when you are teaching. Put students' names on the board to acknowledge use of a word.
Say things like:
Wow! [Isaac] used the word *vanished* when he couldn't find his notebook.

CHAPTER 3 INSTRUCTIONS

Students read pages 13 and 14 with the teacher and pages 15–17 on their own.

COMPREHENSION PROCESSES

Remember, Understand, Apply

PROCEDURES

1. Reviewing Chapters 1 and 2

Identifying—What; Asking Questions; Using Vocabulary—suspense

Quickly discuss the questions from Chapter 2, Setting a Purpose. Say something like:

Yesterday, you read pages 9–12 on your own. Let's see what you found out.

What did Annie and Jack see from the tree house? (They saw a Pteranodon.)

What did the tree house do? (It began spinning, and then it stopped.)

What do you want to find out in Chapter 3? (Where are Jack and Annie?)

That's exactly what I wanted to find out. Where are Jack and Annie?

The author left us up in the air. She left us in . . . suspense!

We know the kids are still in the tree house, but they are in a different oak tree. Let's read Chapter 3 to find out where the oak tree is.

2. Introducing Chapter 3

Identifying—Title; Predicting

Have students read the title.

What's the title of this chapter? (The chapter title is "Where Is Here?")

What do you think we're going to find out in this chapter? (We'll find out where Annie and Jack are now.)

3. First Reading

- Ask questions and discuss the story as indicated by the blue text in this teacher's guide.
- Mix group and individual turns, independent of your voice.
  Have students work toward a group accuracy goal of 0–3 errors.
  Quietly keep track of errors made by all students in the group.
- After reading the story, practice any difficult words.
  Reread the story if students have not reached the accuracy goal.

4. Second Reading, Short Passage Practice: Developing Prosody

- Demonstrate expressive, fluent reading of the first few paragraphs.
  Read at a rate slightly faster than the students' rate.
- Guide practice with your voice.
- Provide individual turns while others track with their fingers and whisper read.
- Repeat with one paragraph or page at a time.

CORRECTING DECODING ERRORS

During story reading, gently correct any error, then have students reread the sentence.

REPEATED READINGS
Prosody

On the second reading, students practice developing prosody— phrasing and expression. Research has shown that prosody is related to both fluency and comprehension.

3
Where Is Here?

Jack looked out the window.

He looked down at the picture in the book.

He looked back out the window.

The world outside and the world in the picture—they were exactly the same.

The Pteranodon was soaring through the sky. The ground was covered with ferns and tall grass. There was a winding stream. A sloping hill. And volcanoes in the distance.

"Wh—where are we?" stammered Jack.

The Pteranodon glided down to the base of their tree. The creature coasted to a stop. And

13

stood very still.

"What happened to us?" said Annie. She looked at Jack. He looked at her.

"I don't know," said Jack. "I was looking at the picture in the book—"

"And you said, 'Wow, I wish I could see a Pteranodon for real,' " said Annie.

"Yeah. And then we saw one. In the Frog Creek woods," said Jack.

"Yeah. And then the wind got loud. And the tree house started spinning," said Annie.

"And we landed here," said Jack.

"And we landed here," said Annie.

"So that means . . ." said Jack.

"So that means . . . what?" said Annie.

"Nothing," said Jack. He shook his head. "None of this can be real."

Annie looked out the window again. "But *he's* real," she said. "He's *very* real."

14

After Reading Page 13

❶ **Understand:** Describing
What did Jack see out the window?
(He saw a Pteranodon, ferns, tall grass, a winding stream, a sloping hill, and volcanoes in the distance.)

❷ **Understand:** Describing
What did Jack see in the book?
(He saw a Pteranodon, ferns, tall grass, a winding stream, a sloping hill, and volcanoes in the distance.)

❸ **Apply:** Inferring, Explaining
Where do you think Jack and Annie are?
(They're in a place just like the book.)

After Reading Page 14

❶ **Apply:** Inferring, Explaining
Do you think Jack and Annie are still in Frog Creek, Pennsylvania? Why or why not?
(They're not in Frog Creek any more. There are no Pteranodons in Frog Creek. They're in Frog Creek, but it's a long time ago, before people lived there.)

❷ **Understand:** Sequencing; **Apply:** Inferring
Jack and Annie are trying to figure out what happened to them by going through the sequence of events. First, Jack was looking at the picture in the book. What happened next?
(He said, "Wow, I wish I could see a Pteranodon for real.")

What happened next?
(They saw a Pteranodon.)

What happened after that?
(The tree house started spinning.)

Where did they land?
(They landed in a place that looked like what they saw in the book.)

> **COMPREHENSION BUILDING**
> **(Reminder)**
> Encourage students to answer questions with complete sentences. If students have difficulty comprehending, think aloud with them or reread the portion of the story that answers the question. Repeat the question.

CHAPTER 3 INSTRUCTIONS
Students read pages 15–17 without the teacher, independently or with partners.

COMPREHENSION PROCESSES
Understand

PREP NOTE
Setting a Purpose
Write questions on a chalkboard, white board, or large piece of paper before working with your small group.

PROCEDURES FOR READING ON YOUR OWN

1. **Getting Ready**
   Have students turn to page 15.

2. **Setting a Purpose**

   Explaining; Asking Questions; Using Vocabulary—suspense
   Establish a purpose for reading. Say something like:
   Read the next part to find out more about the Pteranodon.
   As you read the next pages, try to answer these questions:
   • What did Jack learn about Pteranodons?
   • What did Annie do that made Jack nervous?
   • How did Mary Pope Osborne leave you in *suspense* at the end of Chapter 3?
   • What do you want to find out in Chapter 4?

3. **Reading on Your Own: Partner or Whisper Reading**
   • Have students take turns reading every other page with a partner or have students whisper read pages 15–17 on their own.
   • Continue having students track each word with their fingers.

4. **Comprehension and Skill Work**
   Tell students that they will work on their Book Journal and do Comprehension and Skill Activity 3 after they read on their own. Guide practice, as needed. For teacher directions, see pages 49 and 50.

5. **Homework 3: New Passage**

Jack looked out the window with her. The Pteranodon was standing at the base of the oak tree. Like a guard. His giant wings were spread out on either side of him.

"Hi!" Annie shouted.

"Shush!" said Jack. "We're not supposed to be here."

"But where is *here?*" said Annie.

"I don't know," said Jack.

"Hi!" Annie called again to the creature.

The Pteranodon looked up at them.

"Where is *here?*" Annie called down.

"You're nuts. He can't talk," said Jack. "But maybe the book can tell us."

Jack looked down at the book. He read the words under the picture:

> **This flying reptile lived in the Cretaceous period. It vanished 65 million years ago.**

15

No. Impossible. They couldn't have landed in a time 65 million years ago.

"Jack," said Annie. "He's nice."

"Nice?"

"Yeah, I can tell. Let's go down and talk to him."

"Talk to him?"

Annie started down the rope ladder.

"Hey!" shouted Jack.

But Annie kept going.

"Are you crazy?" Jack called.

Annie dropped to the ground. She stepped boldly up to the ancient creature.

ENTRY 3

COMPREHENSION PROCESSES

Remember, Understand, Evaluate, Create

WRITING TRAITS

Ideas and Content
Word Choice
Conventions—Complete Sentence, Capital, Period
Presentation

Identifying—Event
Sentence Completion

Responding; Predicting; Generating
Ideas; Using Vocabulary—ancient

PROCEDURES

For each step, demonstrate and guide practice, as needed. Then have students complete the page independently.

Personal Response: Paragraph Writing—Specific Instructions

• Have students complete the sentence to explain what happened at the end of the chapter.

• Have students write a paragraph predicting what they think will happen next. Encourage students to use the snazzy word "ancient" in their writing. Remind them to start sentences with a capital and end with period. Say something like:

Read the question. (What do you think will happen next?) You get to predict what you think will happen. You can even pretend you are Mary Pope Osborne.

What is that snazzy word that you are going to try to use? (ancient)

What does *ancient* mean? (really, really old)

You can have a lot of fun with your journal entry. For my journal entry I wrote: "In the next chapter, Annie will talk to the ancient creature. She'll try to make the creature her pet. Annie, Jack, and the creature will become good friends. Then they will fly around the world."

I can't wait to see what you predict. Remember, there is no right or wrong answer when you write a journal.

Self-monitoring

Have students check and correct their work.

STORY COMPREHENSION • COMPARE AND CONTRAST MATRIX

COMPREHENSION PROCESSES
Remember, Understand, Analyze

PROCEDURES
For each step, demonstrate and guide practice, as needed. Then have students complete the page independently.

1. **Compare/Contrast: Matrix—Specific Instructions** (Item 1)
   • Have students read the instructions. Discuss what a matrix is and its purpose. Say something like:
   Read the directions for Item 1. (Complete the chart below. It will help you see what was the same and what was different about what Jack saw from the tree house and what he saw in the book.)

   The chart is called a matrix, and it will help you see how things are the same and how they are different. Read the headings.

   The first column shows . . . Things Jack Saw. The second column shows things he saw . . . From the Tree House.
   The third column shows things he saw . . . (In the Book).
   Then in the last column, you'll circle whether these things are the same or different.

   Let's figure out the first row. The first box says . . . living creatures.
   Read the next box in the row. What did Jack see from the tree house?
   (a Pteranodon flying in the sky)
   Read the third box in the row. What did Jack see in the book? (a blank)
   What goes in the blank? (Pteranodon flying in the sky)
   Was that the same or different? (the same)
   Circle "same."
   • Repeat for "plants" and "land," as needed.

2. **Sentence Completion—Basic Instructions** (Item 2)
   Have students read the question and write the answer. If needed, remind them to end sentences with a period.

3. **Selection Response—Specific Instructions** (Item 3)
   Have students read the sentences and check the two ways in which the author created suspense in the story.

Using Graphic Organizer, Comparing/Contrasting

Identifying—What

Drawing Conclusions

Identifying—What Using Vocabulary— suspense

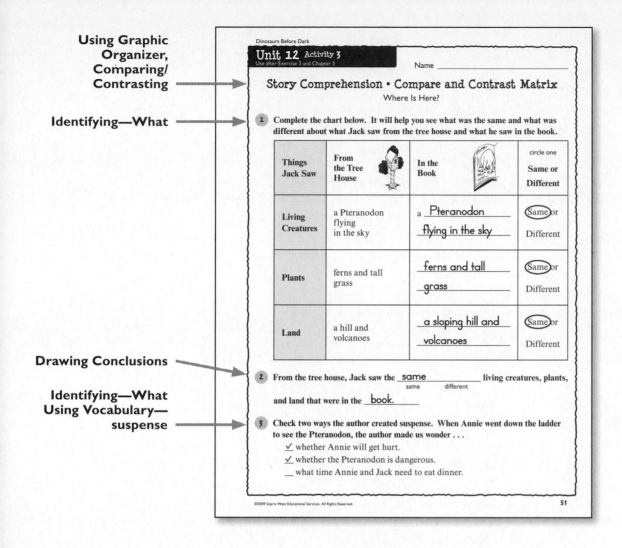

Dinosaurs Before Dark

Unit 12 Activity 3
Use after Exercise 3 and Chapter 3

Name _____

Story Comprehension • Compare and Contrast Matrix
Where Is Here?

1 Complete the chart below. It will help you see what was the same and what was different about what Jack saw from the tree house and what he saw in the book.

Things Jack Saw	From the Tree House	In the Book	circle one Same or Different
Living Creatures	a Pteranodon flying in the sky	a _Pteranodon flying in the sky_	(Same) or Different
Plants	ferns and tall grass	_ferns and tall grass_	(Same) or Different
Land	a hill and volcanoes	_a sloping hill and volcanoes_	(Same) or Different

2 From the tree house, Jack saw the ___same___ living creatures, plants,
                                              same   different
and land that were in the ___book.___

3 Check two ways the author created suspense. When Annie went down the ladder to see the Pteranodon, the author made us wonder . . .
   ✓ whether Annie will get hurt.
   ✓ whether the Pteranodon is dangerous.
   __ what time Annie and Jack need to eat dinner.

51

❶ SOUND REVIEW

Use selected Sound Cards from Units 1–12.

❷ SHIFTY WORD BLENDING

For each word, have students say the underlined sound. Then have them sound out the word smoothly and say it. Use the words in sentences, as appropriate.

❸ SOUND PRACTICE

- For each task, have students spell and say the focus sound in the gray bar. Next, have students read each underlined sound, the word, then the whole column.
- Repeat with each column, building accuracy first, then fluency.

❹ ACCURACY AND FLUENCY BUILDING

- For each task, have students say any underlined part, then read the word.
- Set a pace. Then have students read the whole words in each task and column.
- Provide repeated practice, building accuracy first, then fluency.

C1. Bossy E

Have students identify the underlined sound and then read the word.

D1. Multisyllabic Words

- For the list of words divided by syllables, have students read each syllable, then the whole word. Use the word in a sentence, as appropriate.
- For the list of whole words, build accuracy and then fluency.

probably	If something is likely to happen, you say . . . *probably.*
forward	The opposite of backward is . . . *forward.*
examine	When you study something closely, you . . . *examine* . . . it.
mutant	The plants all grew from the same seed, but one was strange and different. It was a . . . *mutant.*
scientist	An archaeologist is a kind of . . . *scientist.*

E1. Tricky Words

- For each Tricky Word, have students use the sounds and word parts they know to silently sound out the word. Use the word in a sentence to help with pronunciation.
- If the word is unfamiliar, tell students the word.

whole	Taylor didn't want his sandwich cut in half. He wanted it . . . *whole.*
pulled	The door wouldn't open no matter how hard Chara . . . *pulled.*
touch	There was a sign on the dinosaur exhibit that said, "Do not . . . *touch.*"
wonder	My favorite pen disappeared. I . . . *wonder* . . . where it went.

- Have students go back and read the whole words in the column.

❺ MORPHOGRAPHS AND AFFIXES

- Have students read the underlined part, then the word.
- Repeat practice with whole words, mixing group and individual turns. Build accuracy, then fluency.

Dinosaurs Before Dark

Unit 12 Exercise 4
Use before Chapter 4

1. SOUND REVIEW Use selected Sound Cards from Units 1–12.

2. SHIFTY WORD BLENDING For each word, have students say the underlined part, sound out smoothly, then read the word.

f<u>ea</u>st	<u>b</u>east	b<u>e</u>st	<u>r</u>est	<u>cr</u>est

3. SOUND PRACTICE In each column, have students spell and say the sound, then say any underlined sound and the word. Next, have students read the whole column.

gi	ou as in cloud	ea in bread	ai	ci, ce
<u>gi</u>ant	sh<u>ou</u>ted	h<u>ea</u>d	br<u>ai</u>n	pla<u>ce</u>
ima<u>gi</u>ne	c<u>ou</u>nt	br<u>ea</u>th	p<u>ai</u>r	s<u>ci</u>ssors
<u>gi</u>nger	m<u>ou</u>th	alr<u>ea</u>dy	w<u>ai</u>t	pen<u>ci</u>l

4. ACCURACY AND FLUENCY BUILDING For each column, have students say any underlined part, then read each word. Next, have students read the whole column.

A1 New Sound Practice	B1 Mixed Practice	C1 Bossy E	D1 Multisyllabic Words	E1 Tricky Words
f<u>au</u>lt	<u>al</u>ert	wr<u>o</u>te	prob•a•bly	whole
v<u>au</u>lt	l<u>ay</u>er	n<u>o</u>tebook	for•ward	pulled
l<u>au</u>ndry	f<u>ee</u>ls	str<u>o</u>ke	ex•a•mine	touch
A2 Related Words	f<u>or</u>get	str<u>o</u>ked	mu•tant	wonder
c<u>au</u>tion	f<u>u</u>zzy	b<u>o</u>ne	sci•en•tist	**E2** Word Endings
c<u>au</u>tious	huh	b<u>o</u>ny	probably	<u>tilt</u>ed
c<u>au</u>tiously	l<u>ea</u>ned	cl<u>o</u>se	forward	<u>gasp</u>ed
		cl<u>o</u>sing	examine	<u>snort</u>ed
			mutant	
			scientist	

5. MORPHOGRAPHS AND AFFIXES Have students read each underlined part, then the word.

Ⓐ be-	<u>be</u>gan	<u>be</u>ginning	<u>be</u>longs	<u>be</u>tween
Ⓑ laugh<u>able</u>	soft<u>ly</u>	mouth<u>ful</u>	<u>de</u>part	<u>bi</u>weekly

38

CHAPTER 4 INSTRUCTIONS

Students read pages 18–21 with the teacher and pages 22 and 23 on their own.

COMPREHENSION PROCESSES

Remember, Understand, Apply

PROCEDURES

1. **Reviewing Chapter 3**

   Describing—Character Traits (Characterization); Using Vocabulary—curious; Explaining; Asking Questions
   - Discuss the main character. Say something like:
     At the end of Chapter 3, Annie went down the ladder to see the Pteranodon.
     What does that tell you about Annie? (She is brave, bold, and curious . . .)
     Remember those words. You may want to add one or two of the words to your character web in your Book Journal.
   - Discuss the questions from Chapter 3, Setting a Purpose.
     Say something like:
     Yesterday, you read pages 15–17 on your own. Let's see what you found out.
     What did Jack learn about Pteranodons? (He learned that Pteranodons died out 65 million years ago.)
     What did Annie do that made Jack nervous? (She climbed down the ladder and walked up to the Pteranodon.)
     What do you want to learn about in Chapter 4?

2. **Introducing Chapter 4**

   Identifying—Who; Inferring
   Discuss the chapter title.
   This chapter is called "Henry." Who is Henry? (Henry is the neighbor's dog.)
   I wonder why this chapter is called "Henry." What do you think? (The dog will be in the story.)

3. **First Reading**
   - Ask questions and discuss the story as indicated by the blue text in this teacher's guide.
   - Mix group and individual turns, independent of your voice.
     Have students work toward a group accuracy goal of 0–4 errors.
     Quietly keep track of errors made by all students in the group.
   - After reading the story, practice any difficult words.
     Reread the story if students have not reached the accuracy goal.

4. **Second Reading, Timed Readings: Repeated Reading**
   - As time allows, have students do Timed Readings while others follow along.
   - Time individuals for 30 seconds and encourage each child to work for a personal best.
   - Determine words correct per minute. Record student scores.

4

Henry

Jack gasped as Annie held out her hand.

Oh, brother. She was always trying to make friends with animals. But this was going too far.

"Don't get too close to him, Annie!" Jack shouted.

But Annie touched the Pteranodon's crest. She stroked his neck. She was talking to him.

What in the world was she saying?

Jack took a deep breath. Okay. He would go down too. It would be good to examine the

18

creature. Take notes. Like a scientist.

Jack started down the rope ladder.

When he got to the ground, Jack was only a few feet away from the creature.

The creature stared at Jack. His eyes were bright and alert.

"He's soft, Jack," said Annie. "He feels like Henry."

Jack snorted. "He's no dog, Annie."

"Feel him, Jack," said Annie.

Jack didn't move.

"Don't think, Jack. Just do it."

Jack stepped forward. He put out his arm. Very cautiously. He brushed his hand down the creature's neck.

Interesting. A thin layer of fuzz covered the Pteranodon's skin.

"Soft, huh?" said Annie.

Jack reached into his backpack and pulled

19

After Reading Page 18

❶ **Remember:** Identifying—Action
What did Annie do when she climbed down the ladder?
(She touched the Pteranodon's crest, stroked his neck, and talked to him.)

❷ **Apply:** Inferring, Explaining
Do you think the Pteranodon is dangerous? Why or why not?
(The Pteranodon is not dangerous. Annie is touching him, and he's not doing anything.)

After Reading Page 19

❶ **Apply:** Inferring, Explaining
Why do you think Jack went down the ladder?
(He was worried about Annie. He wanted to learn more about the Pteranodon. He didn't want to be left out. He wanted to take notes.)

❷ **Understand:** Describing—Main Character (Characterization); Using Vocabulary—curious
Did you learn anything new about Jack? What?
(At first he seemed afraid. Then he was curious and wanted to take notes . . .)

You may wish to remember some of those things so you can add them to your character web.

out a pencil and a notebook. He wrote:

fuzzy skin

"What are you doing?" asked Annie.

"Taking notes," said Jack. "We're probably the first people in the whole world to ever see a real live Pteranodon."

Jack looked at the Pteranodon again. The creature had a bony crest on top of his head. The crest was longer than Jack's arm.

"I wonder how smart he is," Jack said.

"*Very* smart," said Annie.

"Don't count on it," said Jack. "His brain's probably no bigger than a bean."

"No, he's very smart. I can feel it," said Annie. "I'm going to call him Henry."

Jack wrote in his notebook:

small brain?

20

After Reading Page 20

❶ **Apply:** Inferring, Explaining
Why did Annie name the Pteranodon Henry?
(He feels soft like the dog Henry.)

❷ **Apply:** Inferring; Explaining; Using Vocabulary—extinct
Why does Jack think they are the first people in the world to ever see a Pteranodon?
(Pteranodons are extinct. No one has ever seen a living Pteranodon.)

CHAPTER 4 INSTRUCTIONS

Students read pages 22 and 23 without the teacher, independently or with partners.

COMPREHENSION PROCESSES

Understand, Apply

PREP NOTE
Setting a Purpose
Write questions on a chalkboard, white board, or large piece of paper before working with your small group.

PROCEDURES

1. **Getting Ready**

   Have students turn to page 22.

2. **Setting a Purpose**

   Inferring, Explaining

   Before students begin reading, say something like:

   At the end of the chapter, there's another clue that tells where Annie and Jack are.

   As you read the next pages, try to answer these questions:
   • Why did Annie talk to the Pteranodon?
   • What clue did the author give that tells you where Jack and Annie are?

3. **Reading on Your Own: Partner or Whisper Reading**
   • Have students take turns reading every other page with a partner, or have students whisper read pages 22 and 23 on their own.
   • Continue having students track each word with their fingers.

4. **Comprehension and Skill Work**

   Tell students that they will work on their Book Journal and do Comprehension and Skill Activity 4 after they read on their own. Guide practice, as needed. For teacher directions, see pages 59 and 60.

5. **Homework 4: New Passage**

Jack looked at the creature again. "Maybe he's a mutant," he said.

The creature tilted his head.

Annie laughed. "He's no mutant, Jack."

"Well, what's he doing here then? Where is this place?" said Jack.

Annie leaned close to the Pteranodon.

"Do you know where we are, Henry?" she asked softly.

The creature fixed his eyes on Annie. His long jaws were opening and closing. Like a giant pair of scissors.

"Are you trying to talk to me, Henry?" asked Annie.

"Forget it, Annie." Jack wrote in his notebook:

mouth like scissors?

"Did we come to a time long ago, Henry?"

22

asked Annie. "Is this a place from long ago?" Suddenly she gasped. "Jack!"

He looked up.

Annie was pointing toward the hill. On top stood a huge dinosaur!

23

ENTRY 4

COMPREHENSION PROCESSES

Understand, Evaluate, Create

WRITING TRAITS

Ideas and Content
Word Choice
Conventions—Complete Sentence,
Capital, Period
Presentation

Using Graphic Organizer; Describing—
Character Traits (Characterization)

Responding; Explaining
Generating Ideas; Using Vocabulary—
creature, ancient

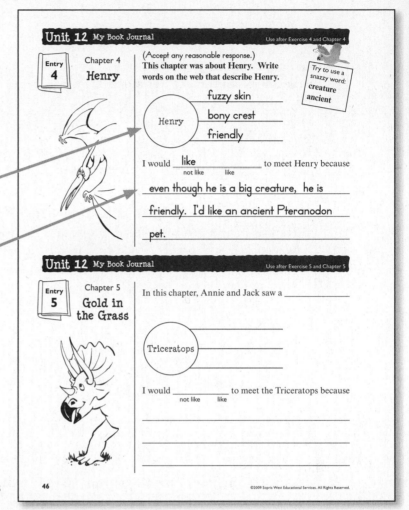

PROCEDURES

For each step, demonstrate and guide practice, as needed. Then have students complete the page independently.

1. Characterization: Web—Specific Instructions

Have students write words or phrases that describe Henry. Say something like:
In Chapter 4, Jack and Annie met a Pteranodon that Annie named Henry. Read the instructions for Entry 4 of your Book Journal.
(This chapter was about Henry. Write words on the web that describe Henry.)
What are some words or phrases that we could write to describe Henry?
(mouth like scissors, fuzzy skin, bony crest, friendly, a Pteranodon)
Yes, these all describe Henry.

2. Characterization: Paragraph Writing—Basic Instructions

• Have students fill in the blank to complete the first sentence, then write a second sentence explaining why they would like or not like to meet Henry. Encourage students to use the snazzy vocabulary words "creature" and "ancient." Remind students to start sentences with a capital and end with a period.

• Think aloud with students and discuss possible answers, as needed.

Self-monitoring

Have students check and correct their work.

STORY COMPREHENSION • NOTE TAKING

COMPREHENSION PROCESSES
Understand, Apply

WRITING TRAITS
Ideas and Content
Conventions—Complete Sentence, Capital, Period
Presentation

PROCEDURES
For each step, demonstrate and guide practice, as needed. Then have students complete the page independently.

1. **Note Taking: Locating Information—Specific Instructions** (Item 1)
   - Have students read the instructions and the topic.
   - For each fact, have students look in their storybook to find the information.
   - Have students read the phrases and fill in the blanks to complete the notes.
     You're going to find information in your storybook about the Pteranodon.
     The story is fiction, but the author has written information that is true.
     Let's complete Fact 1. What page will we look on? (page 9)
     Read the incomplete fact, then turn to page 9 and find the information.
     Thumbs up when you find the fact.
     [Liza], what information did you find to complete that fact? (A Pteranodon has huge bat-like wings.)
     Yes, that's right. So, what word will you write in the blank? (bat-like)
   - Repeat for Facts 2–4, as needed.

2. **Description: Paragraph Writing—Basic Instructions** (Item 2)
   Have students read the instructions and write a paragraph using the notes from Item 1. Remind them to start sentences with a capital and end with a period.

3. **Diagram: Labeling—Basic Instructions** (Item 3)
   Have students follow the directions and label the parts of the Pteranodon. Assist, as needed.

Self-monitoring
Have students check and correct their work.

Locating Information
Describing
Identifying

Describing
Using—Facts

Using Graphic
Organizer, Following
Directions

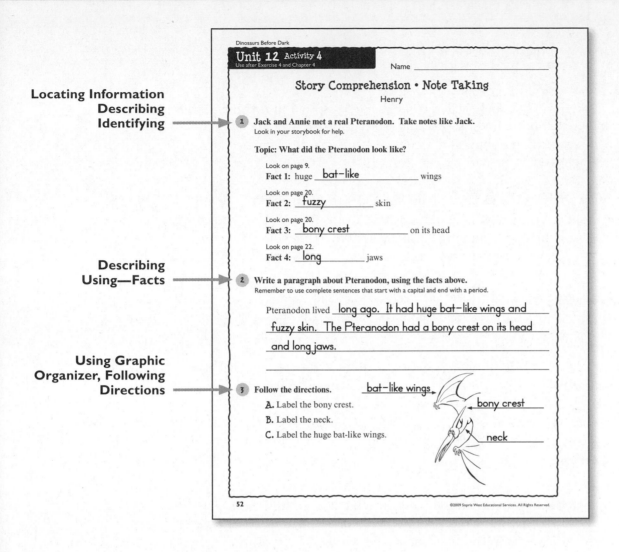

Dinosaurs Before Dark

Unit 12 Activity 4
Use after Exercise 4 and Chapter 4

Name _____

Story Comprehension • Note Taking
Henry

1 Jack and Annie met a real Pteranodon. Take notes like Jack.
Look in your storybook for help.

Topic: What did the Pteranodon look like?

Look on page 9.
Fact 1: huge ___bat-like___ wings

Look on page 20.
Fact 2: ___fuzzy___ skin

Look on page 20.
Fact 3: ___bony crest___ on its head

Look on page 22.
Fact 4: ___long___ jaws

2 Write a paragraph about Pteranodon, using the facts above.
Remember to use complete sentences that start with a capital and end with a period.

Pteranodon lived ___long ago. It had huge bat-like wings and___
___fuzzy skin. The Pteranodon had a bony crest on its head___
___and long jaws.___

_____

3 Follow the directions.
   A. Label the bony crest.
   B. Label the neck.
   C. Label the huge bat-like wings.

bat-like wings

bony crest

neck

52

❶ SOUND REVIEW

Use selected Sound Cards from Units 1–12.

❷ SOUND PRACTICE

- For each task, have students spell and say the focus sound in the gray bar. Next, have students read each underlined sound, the word, then the whole column.
- Repeat with each column, building accuracy first, then fluency.

❸ ACCURACY AND FLUENCY BUILDING

- For each task, have students say any underlined part, then read the word.
- Set a pace. Then have students read the whole words in each task and column.
- Provide repeated practice, building accuracy first, then fluency.

B1. Multisyllabic Words

- For the list of words divided by syllables, have students read each syllable, then the whole word. Use the word in a sentence, as appropriate.
- For the list of whole words, build accuracy and then fluency.

fancy	Her dress was plain, not . . . *fancy.*
caption	The sentence beside a picture that tells about the picture is a . . . *caption.*
incredibly	He was very, very grateful. He was . . . *incredibly* . . . grateful.
finger	Vicki wears a ring on her pinkie . . . *finger.*
cheerfully	Tom was happy to hand out homework. He handed it out . . . *cheerfully.*
engraved	The trophy had the winner's name . . . *engraved* . . . on it.
glittering	The diamond jewelry was . . . *glittering.*

D1. Tricky Words

- For each Tricky Word, have students use the sounds and word parts they know to silently sound out the word. Use the word in a sentence to help with pronunciation.
- If the word is unfamiliar, tell students the word.

magnolia	My favorite kind of tree is a . . . *magnolia.*
medallion	For winning the state science contest, each student received a . . . *medallion.*
shoulder	Patrice threw the ball so hard it hurt his . . . *shoulder.*
half	Please cut my apple in . . . *half.*
weighed	He stepped on the scale so he could be . . . *weighed.*
period	Many different kinds of dinosaurs lived during the Jurassic . . . *period.*
view	I looked out the window and saw the beautiful ocean . . . *view.*

- Have students go back and read the whole words in the column.

❹ WORD ENDINGS

Have students read any underlined word, then the word with an ending.

❺ DINOSAUR WORDS

Have students read the word, using the pronunciation guide for help, then the sentence.

❻ GENERALIZATION: READING NEW WORDS IN PARAGRAPHS

- Have students read the paragraph silently, then out loud. Tell students to use the sounds and word parts they know to read any difficult words.
- Repeat practice, as needed.

Dinosaurs Before Dark

Unit 12 Exercise 5
Use before Chapter 5

1. SOUND REVIEW Use selected Sound Cards from Units 1–12.

2. SOUND PRACTICE In each column, have students spell and say the sound, then say any underlined sound and the word. Next, have students read the whole column.

au	-dge, ge	kn	ew	ea as in bread
c<u>au</u>tion	nu<u>dge</u>d	<u>kn</u>elt	bl<u>ew</u>	h<u>ea</u>d
astron<u>au</u>t	pa<u>ge</u>s	<u>kn</u>eeled	thr<u>ew</u>	br<u>ea</u>th
f<u>au</u>lt	hu<u>ge</u>	<u>kn</u>ow	kn<u>ew</u>	inst<u>ea</u>d

3. ACCURACY AND FLUENCY BUILDING For each column, have students say any underlined part, then read each word. Next, have students read the whole column.

A1 Mixed Practice	B1 Multisyllabic Words		C1 Shifty Words	D1 Tricky Words
q<u>ui</u>t	fan•cy	fancy	fl<u>i</u>pped	magnolia
b<u>ye</u>	cap•tion	caption	<u>sl</u>ipped	medallion
<u>oo</u>ps	in•cred•i•bly	incredibly	slapped	shoulder
lips	fin•ger	finger		half
f<u>er</u>ns	cheer•ful•ly	cheerfully	r<u>o</u>pe	weighed
g<u>o</u>ld	en•graved	engraved	l<u>o</u>pe	period
sl<u>u</u>ng	glit•ter•ing	glittering	<u>sl</u>ope	view

4. WORD ENDINGS Have students read each word, then the word with an ending.

A	<u>lop</u>ed	<u>grunt</u>ed	<u>slam</u>med	<u>calm</u>ly	<u>pant</u>ing
B	tease	teasing	ignore	ignored	tumble	tumbled

5. DINOSAUR WORDS Have students use the sounds and word parts they know and the pronunciation guide to read the words. Then have them read the sentence.

Triceratops	Try-sair-uh-tops	<u>Triceratops</u> was a plant eater.

6. GENERALIZATION Have students read the paragraph silently, then out loud. (New words: rhinoceros, shield, horn)

Last Sunday, Mom took my little brother and me to the drive-through wildlife park. We drove by a big rhinoceros. My little brother said, "If it had a shield and another horn, it would look like a Triceratops!"

Mom said, "A Triceratops! You sure have a good imagination!"

39

> **GRADUALLY INCREASE STUDENT RESPONSE RATE (Reminder)**
>
> After students are accurate, gradually increase the rate of response. Demonstrate and guide a pace slightly faster than the students' rate.

COMPREHENSION PROCESSES

Understand, Apply

PROCEDURES

Introducing Vocabulary

★**caption** ★**medallion** ★**engraved** ★**bellow** ★**bellowing** ★**start after**

- For each vocabulary word, have students read the word by parts, then read the whole word.
- Read the student-friendly explanations to students as they follow with their fingers. Then have students use the vocabulary word by following the gray text.
- Review and discuss the illustrations.

  Note: Student vocabulary pages for this unit are found in the students' *Exercise Book 2*.

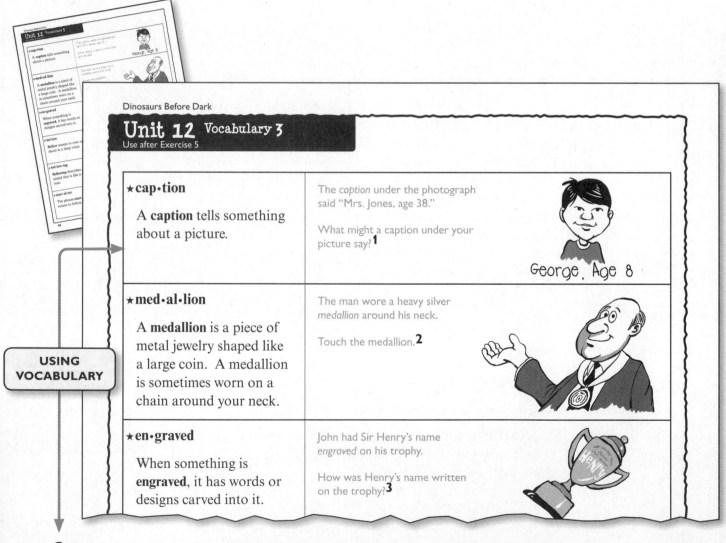

Dinosaurs Before Dark

Unit 12 Vocabulary 3
Use after Exercise 5

USING VOCABULARY

★**cap·tion** A **caption** tells something about a picture.	The *caption* under the photograph said "Mrs. Jones, age 38." What might a caption under your picture say?**1**
★**med·al·lion** A **medallion** is a piece of metal jewelry shaped like a large coin. A medallion is sometimes worn on a chain around your neck.	The man wore a heavy silver *medallion* around his neck. Touch the medallion.**2**
★**en·graved** When something is **engraved**, it has words or designs carved into it.	John had Sir Henry's name *engraved* on his trophy. How was Henry's name written on the trophy?**3**

George, Age 8

❶ **Apply:** Using Vocabulary—caption (Joe Benton, age 8; Lana Yang, superhero . . .)

❷ **Apply:** Demonstrating; Using Vocabulary—medallion

❸ **Apply:** Using Vocabulary—engraved (It was engraved on it.)

★ = New in this unit

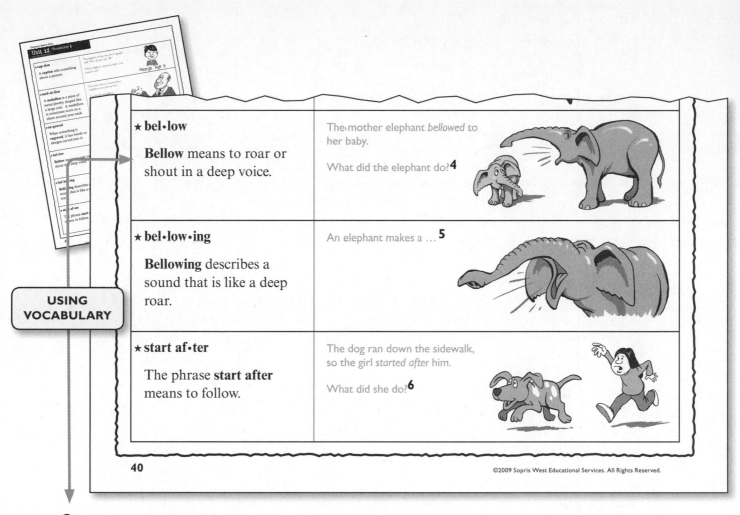

USING
VOCABULARY

★ **bel·low**

Bellow means to roar or shout in a deep voice.

The mother elephant *bellowed* to her baby.

What did the elephant do?**4**

★ **bel·low·ing**

Bellowing describes a sound that is like a deep roar.

An elephant makes a … **5**

★ **start af·ter**

The phrase **start after** means to follow.

The dog ran down the sidewalk, so the girl *started after* him.

What did she do?**6**

40

❹ **Apply:** Using Vocabulary—bellow (The mother elephant bellowed.)

❺ **Apply:** Using Vocabulary—bellowing (bellowing sound)

❻ **Understand:** Using Idioms and Expressions—start after (She followed him.)

USING VOCABULARY

Be enthusiastic about learning new words. Keep a running list of words you would like to use and encourage students to use. Keep the list handy when you are teaching. Put students' names on the board to acknowledge use of a word.
Say things like:
Wow! [Anasi] used the word *caption* when she talked about the picture.

CHAPTER 5 INSTRUCTIONS
Students read pages 24–26 with the teacher and pages 27–32 on their own.

COMPREHENSION PROCESSES
Remember, Understand, Apply

PROCEDURES

1. Reviewing Chapter 4

Identifying—What; Inferring; Explaining

- Have students quickly review what happened in Chapter 4.
  Say something like:
  In Chapter 4, Annie and Jack met a Pteranodon.
  Annie treated the Pteranodon like a pet dog. What did she do? (She petted it and talked to it.)

- Discuss the questions from Chapter 4, Setting a Purpose.
  Say something like:
  Yesterday, you read pages 22 and 23 on your own. Let's see what you found out.
  Why did Annie talk to the Pteranodon? (She thought it might tell her where they were.)
  What clue did the author give that tells you where Jack and Annie are?
  (There's another dinosaur. It makes you think the kids have traveled across time to when the dinosaurs lived.)

2. Introducing Chapter 5

Identifying—Title
Have students identify the chapter. Say something like:
What's the title of this chapter? (Gold in the Grass)

3. First Reading
- Ask questions and discuss the story as indicated by the blue text in this teacher's guide.
- Mix group and individual turns, independent of your voice.
  Have students work toward a group accuracy goal of 0–4 errors.
  Quietly keep track of errors made by all students in the group.
- After reading the story, practice any difficult words.
  Repeat if students have not reached the accuracy goal.

4. Second Reading, Short Passage Practice: Developing Prosody
- Demonstrate expressive, fluent reading of the first paragraph. Read at a rate slightly faster than the students' rate.
- Guide practice with your voice.
- Provide individual turns while others track with their fingers and whisper read.
  Provide descriptive and positive feedback.
- Repeat with one paragraph or one page at a time.

> **CORRECTING DECODING ERRORS**
> During story reading, gently correct any error, then have students reread the sentence.

5

Gold in the Grass

"Go! *Go!*" said Jack. He threw his notebook into his pack. He pushed Annie toward the rope ladder.

"Bye, Henry!" she said.

"Go!" said Jack. He gave Annie a big push.

"Quit it!" she said. But she started up the ladder. Jack scrambled after her.

They tumbled into the tree house.

They were panting as they looked out the window at the dinosaur. He was standing on the hilltop. Eating flowers off a tree.

24

"Oh, man," whispered Jack. "We *are* in a time long ago!"

The dinosaur looked like a huge rhinoceros. Only he had three horns instead of one. Two long ones above his eyes and one on his nose. He had a big shield-like thing behind his head.

"Triceratops!" said Jack.

"Does he eat people?" whispered Annie.

"I'll look it up." Jack grabbed the dinosaur book. He flipped through the pages.

"There!" he said. He pointed to a picture of a Triceratops. He read the caption:

> **The Triceratops lived in the late Cretaceous period. This plant-eating dinosaur weighed over 12,000 pounds.**

Jack slammed the book shut. "Just plants. No meat."

"Let's go see him," said Annie.

25

After Reading Page 24

❶ **Apply:** Inferring, Explaining
The dinosaur is probably an herbivore. How do you know?
(It's eating flowers off a tree.)

After Reading Page 25

❶ **Apply:** Inferring; Explaining; Using Vocabulary—extinct
Why does Jack think he's in a time long ago?
(Jack and Annie see a Triceratops. Dinosaurs became extinct 65 million years ago.)

❷ **Apply:** Inferring, Explaining
Why did Annie think it was safe to go see the dinosaur?
(The Triceratops doesn't eat meat, so she didn't think it would hurt her.)

❸ **Understand:** Summarizing
Jack looked in the dinosaur book to find out about the Triceratops. What facts did he learn?
(It lived in the late Cretaceous period. It was a plant eater. It weighed over 12,000 pounds.)

"Are you nuts?" said Jack.

"Don't you want to take notes about him?" asked Annie. "We're probably the first people in the whole world to ever see a real live Triceratops."

Jack sighed. She was right.

"Let's go," he said.

He shoved the dinosaur book into his pack. He slung it over his shoulder and started down the ladder.

On the way down, Jack stopped.

He called up to Annie, "Just promise you won't pet him."

"I promise."

"Promise you won't kiss him."

"I promise."

"Promise you won't talk to him."

"I promise."

"Promise you won't—"

26

After Reading Page 26

❶ **Apply:** Inferring, Explaining
How did Annie convince Jack to go see the dinosaur?
(She asked him if he wanted to take notes. She reminded him that they were probably the first people to ever see a Triceratops.)

CHAPTER 5 INSTRUCTIONS

Students read pages 27–32 without the teacher, independently or with partners.

COMPREHENSION PROCESSES

Remember, Understand, Apply

PROCEDURES

1. Getting Ready

Have students turn to page 27.

2. Setting a Purpose

Identifying—Where; Summarizing; Inferring; Explaining

Before students begin reading, say something like:

As you read the rest of the chapter, try to answer the following questions.

- Where was the Pteranodon?
- What did Annie and Jack learn about the Triceratops in this story?
- What was the gold in the grass? Why is it important?

3. Reading on Your Own: Partner or Whisper Reading

- Have students take turns reading every other page with a partner, or have students whisper read pages 27–32 on their own.
- Continue having students track each word with their fingers.

4. Comprehension and Skill Work

Tell students that they will work on their Book Journal and do Comprehension and Skill Activity 5 after they read on their own. Guide practice, as needed. For teacher directions, see pages 73 and 74.

5. Homework 5: New Passage

PREP NOTE

Setting a Purpose

Write questions on a chalkboard, white board, or large piece of paper before working with your small group.

OPTIONAL MID-UNIT ASSESSMENT

For students who require careful monitoring (lowest-performing students in the group), give the mid-unit Oral Reading Fluency Assessment found on page 138.

"Go! Go!" she said.

Jack went.

Annie followed.

When they stepped off the ladder, the Pteranodon gave them a kind look.

Annie blew a kiss at him. "Be back soon, Henry," she said cheerfully.

"Shush!" said Jack. And he led the way through the ferns. Slowly and carefully.

When he reached the bottom of the hill, he kneeled behind a fat bush.

Annie knelt beside him and started to speak.

"Shush!" Jack put his finger to his lips.

Annie made a face.

Jack peeked out at the Triceratops.

The dinosaur was incredibly big. Bigger than a truck. He was eating the flowers off a magnolia tree.

27

Jack slipped his notebook out of his pack. He wrote:

eats flowers

Annie nudged him.

Jack ignored her. He studied the Triceratops again. He wrote:

eats slowly

Annie nudged him hard.

Jack looked at her.

Annie pointed to herself. She walked her fingers through the air. She pointed to the dinosaur. She smiled.

Was she teasing?

She waved at Jack.

Jack started to grab her.

She laughed and jumped away. She fell into the grass. In full view of the Triceratops!

28

70

"Get back!" whispered Jack.

Too late. The big dinosaur had spotted Annie. He gazed down at her from the hilltop. Half of a magnolia flower was sticking out of his mouth.

"Oops," said Annie.

"Get back!" Jack shouted at her.

"He looks nice, Jack."

"Nice? Watch out for his horns, Annie!"

"No. He's nice, Jack."

Nice?

But the Triceratops just gazed calmly down at Annie. Then he turned and loped away. Down the side of the hill.

"Bye!" said Annie. She turned back to Jack. "See?"

Jack grunted. But he wrote in his notebook:

nice

29

"Come on. Let's look around some more," said Annie.

As Jack started after Annie, he saw something glittering in the tall grass. He reached out and picked it up.

A medallion. A gold medallion.

31

A letter was engraved on the medallion. A fancy M.

"Oh, man. Someone came here before us," Jack said softly.

32

ENTRY 5

COMPREHENSION PROCESSES

Remember, Understand, Evaluate

WRITING TRAITS

Ideas and Content
Word Choice
Conventions—Complete Sentence,
Capital, Period
Presentation

Identifying—What

Using Graphic Organizer; Describing

Responding, Explaining

PROCEDURES

For each step, demonstrate and guide practice, as needed. Then have students complete the page independently.

1. Characterization: Web—Specific Instructions
• Have students complete the sentence to identify what Annie and Jack saw.
• Have students write words or phrases that describe the Triceratops.

2. Characterization: Paragraph Writing—Specific Instructions
• Have students fill in the blank to complete the first sentence, then write a second sentence explaining why they would like or not like to meet the Triceratops. Encourage students to use snazzy vocabulary words in their writing. Remind students to start sentences with a capital and end with a period.
• Think aloud with students and discuss possible answers, as needed.

Self-monitoring
Have students check and correct their work.

STORY COMPREHENSION • NOTE TAKING

COMPREHENSION PROCESSES
Understand, Apply

WRITING TRAITS
Conventions—Complete Sentence, Capital, Period, Quotation Marks

PROCEDURES
For each step, demonstrate and guide practice, as needed. Then have students complete the page independently.

1. **Note Taking: Locating Information—Basic Instructions** (Item 1)
   - For each fact, have students look in their book and find the information.
   - Have students read the phrases and fill in the blanks to complete the facts.

2. **Caption: Sentence Writing—Specific Instructions** (Item 2)
   - Have students read the instructions and write a caption, using the notes from Item 1.
   Read the instructions for Item 2. (Write a caption about Triceratops.)
   A caption is a short explanation or description of an illustration or photograph.
   Put your finger on the illustration. What are you going to write a caption about? (Triceratops)
   The caption has been started for you.
   Read the beginning of the caption. (Triceratops was . . .)
   You know a lot about Triceratops from your fact list.

   - Model or, if time allows, have partners discuss what they might write.
   Say something like:
   Partner 1, tell your partner what you might write about Triceratops. Remember, a caption is short.
   After about a minute say: Partner Two, your turn.
   After about a minute say: Let's share some of the captions you talked about.

   - Have students write a caption using their own words.
   Remind them to end sentences with a period.

3. **Following Directions** (Item 3)

4. **Selection Response—Basic Instructions** (Item 4)
   Have students read the sentences, then fill in the bubble for the correct answer.

Self-monitoring
Have students check and correct their work.

**Locating Information
Describing
Identifying—Facts**

**Summarizing
Describing; Using
Vocabulary—caption**

Following Directions

**Using Vocabulary—
medallion, suspense,
curious**

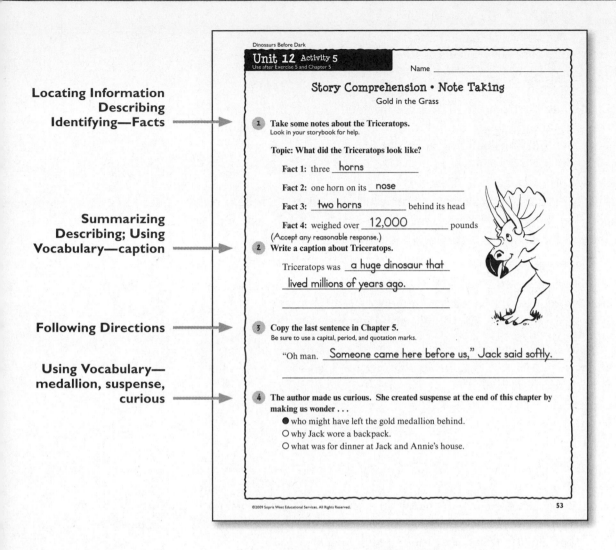

Dinosaurs Before Dark

Unit 12 Activity 5
Use after Exercise 5 and Chapter 5

Name _____

Story Comprehension • Note Taking
Gold in the Grass

1 Take some notes about the Triceratops.
Look in your storybook for help.

Topic: What did the Triceratops look like?

Fact 1: three __horns__

Fact 2: one horn on its __nose__

Fact 3: __two horns__ behind its head

Fact 4: weighed over __12,000__ pounds
(Accept any reasonable response.)

2 Write a caption about Triceratops.

Triceratops was __a huge dinosaur that__
__lived millions of years ago.__
_____

3 Copy the last sentence in Chapter 5.
Be sure to use a capital, period, and quotation marks.

"Oh man. __Someone came here before us,__" Jack said softly.
_____

4 The author made us curious. She created suspense at the end of this chapter by
making us wonder . . .
● who might have left the gold medallion behind.
○ why Jack wore a backpack.
○ what was for dinner at Jack and Annie's house.

53

❶ SOUND REVIEW

Use selected Sound Cards from Units 1–12.

❷ SOUND PRACTICE

- For each task, have students spell and say the focus sound in the gray bar. Next, have students read each underlined sound, the word, then the whole column.
- Repeat with each column, building accuracy first, then fluency.

❸ ACCURACY AND FLUENCY BUILDING

- For each task, have students say any underlined part, then read the word.
- Set a pace. Then have students read the whole words in each task and column.
- Provide repeated practice, building accuracy first, then fluency.

C1. Multisyllabic Words

- For the list of words divided by syllables, have students read each syllable, then the whole word. Use the word in a sentence, as appropriate.
- For the list of whole words, build accuracy and then fluency.

attention	The teacher said . . . *"Attention . . .* please!"
bellowing	I wish my dog would stop howling and . . . *bellowing!*
valley	The dinosaurs headed for the lush . . . *valley.*
examined	She studied the plant closely. She . . . *examined . . .* it.
tuba	Jason wanted to play the . . . *tuba.*
dangling	He tried to get the horse to follow him by . . . *dangling . . .* a carrot in front of it.

D1. Tricky Words

- For each Tricky Word, have students use the sounds and word parts they know to silently sound out the word. Use the word in a sentence to help with pronunciation.
- If the word is unfamiliar, tell students the word.

sorry	He apologized. He said he was . . . *sorry.*
magnolia	Can you smell the sweet blossoms on that . . . *magnolia . . .* tree?
mothers	The lion cubs all stayed close to their . . . *mothers.*
come	Sasha will . . . *come . . .* to my house tomorrow.
comes	Sasha . . . *comes . . .* to my house every day.
coming	Sasha is . . . *coming . . .* to my house right now.

- Have students go back and read the whole words in the column.

❹ WORD ENDINGS

Have students read the underlined word, then the word with an ending.

❺ DINOSAUR WORDS

- Have students read each word, using the pronunciation guide for help.
- Use the word in a sentence, as needed.

❻ GENERALIZATION: READING NEW WORDS IN PARAGRAPHS

- Have students read the paragraph silently, then out loud. Tell students to use the sounds and word parts they know to read any difficult words.
- Repeat practice, as needed.

Dinosaurs Before Dark

Unit 12 Exercise 6
Use before Chapter 6

1. SOUND REVIEW Use selected Sound Cards from Units 1–12.

2. SOUND PRACTICE In each column, have students spell and say the sound, then say any underlined sound and the word. Next, have students read the whole column.

au	ea as in bread	gi	be-	ow as in cow
c<u>au</u>se	br<u>ea</u>th	<u>i</u>magine	<u>be</u>cause	h<u>ow</u>
c<u>aug</u>ht	h<u>ea</u>ds	<u>gi</u>ant	<u>be</u>gin	b<u>ow</u>
exh<u>au</u>st	alr<u>ea</u>dy	<u>gi</u>gantic	<u>be</u>came	b<u>ow</u>ed

3. ACCURACY AND FLUENCY BUILDING For each column, have students say any underlined part, then read each word. Next, have students read the whole column.

A1 Mixed Practice	B1 Bossy E	C1 Multisyllabic Words		D1 Tricky Words
j<u>ea</u>ns	fr<u>o</u>ze	at·ten·tion	attention	sorry
<u>ug</u>ly	fr<u>o</u>zen	bel·low·ing	bellowing	magnolia
f<u>ar</u>ther	s<u>a</u>ve	val·ley	valley	mothers
barg<u>ed</u>	s<u>a</u>ving	ex·a·mined	examined	
ch<u>ew</u>		tu·ba	tuba	come
p<u>ay</u>ing	r<u>a</u>ce	dang·ling	dangling	comes
	r<u>a</u>ced			coming

4. WORD ENDINGS Have students read each word, then the word with an ending.

Ⓐ	to<u>pp</u>ed	stuff<u>ed</u>	<u>h</u>unted	mutter<u>ed</u>
Ⓑ	swin<u>g</u>ing	crawl<u>ing</u>	tower<u>ing</u>	crouch<u>ing</u>

5. DINOSAUR WORDS Have students use the sounds and word parts they know and the pronunciation guide to read the words.

Tyrannosaurus	Tuh-ran-uh-sore-us	Anatosaurus	Uh-nat-uh-sore-us

6. GENERALIZATION Have students read the paragraph silently, then out loud. (New words: shriek, waddled, afraid, gleaming, pocket)

    Annie let out a shriek as the terrible duck-billed monster waddled toward her. She was afraid of its gleaming green eyes. She pulled the magic medallion out of her pocket and made a wish. Suddenly, the monster turned into a beautiful bird. Then she heard a kind voice, "Don't be afraid. I am your friend."

41

CHAPTER 6 INSTRUCTIONS

Students read pages 33–37 with the teacher and pages 38–42 on their own.

COMPREHENSION PROCESSES

Remember, Understand, Apply

PROCEDURES

1. Reviewing Chapter 5

Identifying—Where; Summarizing; Inferring; Explaining; Using Vocabulary—medallion, engraved

Quickly discuss the questions from Chapter 5, Setting a Purpose.
Say something like:
Yesterday, you read pages 27–32 on your own. Let's see what you found out.
In Chapter 5, where was the Pteranodon? (It was hanging out near the tree house.)
What did Annie and Jack learn about the Triceratops in this story? (It was a plant eater, weighed 12,000 pounds, lived in the late Cretaceous period, had three horns, ate slowly, and was nice.)
What was the gold in the grass? (It was a gold medallion engraved with the letter M.)
Why is it important? (It meant someone else had been in the land of the dinosaurs.)

2. Introducing Chapter 6

Identifying—Title, When, How Many
What's the title of the chapter? (Dinosaur Valley)
Jack and Annie have traveled back in time. When did the dinosaurs live? (They lived 65 million years ago.)
So Jack and Annie are in the time of the dinosaurs—how many years ago? (65 million years ago)

3. First Reading

- Ask questions and discuss the story as indicated by the blue text in this teacher's guide.
- Mix group and individual turns, independent of your voice.
  Have students work toward a group accuracy goal of 0–5 errors.
  Quietly keep track of errors made by all students in the group.
- After reading the story, practice any difficult words.
  Reread the story if students have not reached the accuracy goal.

4. Second Reading, Timed Readings: Repeated Reading

- As time allows, have students do Timed Readings while others follow along.
- Time individuals for 30 seconds and encourage each child to work for a personal best.
- Determine words correct per minute. Record student scores.

6

Dinosaur Valley

"Annie, look at this!" Jack called. "Look what I found!"

Annie had gone up to the hilltop.

She was busy picking a flower from the magnolia tree.

"Annie, look! A medallion!"

But Annie wasn't paying attention to Jack. She was staring at something on the other side of the hill.

"Oh, wow!" she said.

"Annie!"

33

Clutching her magnolia flower, she took off down the hill.

"Annie, come back!" Jack shouted.

But Annie had disappeared.

"I'm going to kill her," Jack muttered.

He stuffed the gold medallion into his jeans pocket.

Then he heard Annie shriek.

"Annie?"

Jack heard another sound as well. A deep, bellowing sound. Like a tuba.

"Jack! Come here!" Annie called.

"Annie!"

Jack grabbed his backpack and raced up the hill.

When he got to the top, he gasped.

The valley below was filled with nests. Big nests made out of mud. And the nests were filled with tiny dinosaurs!

34

After Reading Page 33

❶ **Remember:** Identifying—What; Using Vocabulary—medallion
What did Jack want to show Annie?
(Jack wanted to show Annie the medallion.)

❷ **Understand:** Explaining
Why wasn't Annie paying attention?
(She was staring at something on the other side of the hill.)

After Reading Page 34

❶ **Understand:** Describing
Describe what was on the other side of the hill.
(There were dinosaur nests filled with tiny dinosaurs.)

❷ **Apply:** Inferring; Explaining; Using Vocabulary—amazed
The book doesn't tell you, but how do you think Jack and Annie felt? Why?
(They were excited and amazed because they had never seen dinosaur babies. No one had ever seen real dinosaur babies. Annie probably thought the babies were cute . . .)

Annie was crouching next to one of the nests. And standing over her was a gigantic duck-billed dinosaur!

"Don't panic. Don't move," said Jack. He stepped slowly down the hill toward Annie.

The huge dinosaur was towering above Annie. Waving her arms. Making her tuba sound.

Jack stopped. He didn't want to get too close.

He knelt on the ground. "Okay. Move toward me. Slowly," he said.

Annie started to stand up.

"Don't stand. Crawl," said Jack.

Clutching her flower, Annie crawled toward Jack.

The duck-billed dinosaur followed her. Still bellowing.

Annie froze.

36

After Reading Page 36

❶ **Apply:** Inferring; Explaining; Using Vocabulary—protect
Why do you think the duck-billed dinosaur started following Annie?
(It was the mother dinosaur, and she was protecting her babies.)

❷ **Apply:** Inferring, Explaining
Why do you think Annie froze?
(She was scared.)

"Keep going," Jack said softly.

Annie started crawling again.

Jack inched farther down the hill. Until he was just an arm's distance from Annie.

He reached out—and grabbed her hand.

He pulled Annie toward him.

"Stay down," he said. He crouched next to her. "Bow your head. Pretend to chew."

"Chew?"

"Yes. I read that's what you do if a mean dog comes at you."

"She's no dog, Jack," said Annie.

"Just chew," said Jack.

Jack and Annie both bowed their heads. And pretended to chew.

Soon the dinosaur grew quiet.

Jack raised his head.

"I don't think she's mad anymore," he said.

"Thanks, Jack, for saving me," said Annie.

37

After Reading Page 37

❶ **Understand:** Explaining
How did Jack save Annie?
(He told Annie to bow her head and chew. The dinosaur quit being mad.)

CHAPTER 6 INSTRUCTIONS
Students read pages 38–42 without the teacher, independently or with partners.

PREP NOTE
Setting a Purpose
Write questions on a chalk board, white board, or large piece of paper before working with your small group.

COMPREHENSION PROCESSES
Remember, Understand, Apply

PROCEDURES

1. **Getting Ready**
   Have students turn to page 38.

2. **Setting a Purpose**

   Identifying—What, Where; Inferring; Explaining; Using Vocabulary— suspense
   Before students begin reading, say something like:
   As you read the rest of the chapter, try to answer the following questions. When you are done, stop and think about the questions with your partner.
   • What did Jack read about the duck-billed dinosaur?
   • Where were the other mother dinosaurs?
   • The book doesn't tell, but what do you think it means when the dinosaur makes the tuba sound?
   • At the end of the chapter, the author builds suspense. What does Jack see?

3. **Reading on Your Own: Partner or Whisper Reading**
   • Have students take turns reading every other page with a partner, or have students whisper read pages 38–42 on their own.
   • Continue having students track each word with their fingers.

4. **Comprehension and Skill Work**
   Tell students that they will work on their Book Journal and do Comprehension and Skill Activities 6 and 7 after they read on their own. Guide practice, as needed. For teacher directions, see pages 86–88.

5. **Homework 6: New Passage**

"You have to use your brain," said Jack. "You can't just go running to a nest of babies. There's always a mother nearby."

Annie stood up.

"Annie!"

Too late.

Annie held out her magnolia flower to the dinosaur.

"I'm sorry I made you worry about your babies," she said.

The dinosaur moved closer to Annie. She grabbed the flower from her. She reached for another.

"No more," said Annie.

The dinosaur let out a sad tuba sound.

"But there are more flowers up there," Annie said. She pointed to the top of the hill. "I'll get you some."

Annie hurried up the hill.

38

The dinosaur waddled after her.

Jack quickly examined the babies. Some were crawling out of their nests.

Where were the other mothers?

Jack took out the dinosaur book. He flipped through the pages.

He found a picture of some duck-billed dinosaurs. He read the caption:

The Anatosauruses lived in colonies. While a few mothers baby-sat the nests, others hunted for food.

So there must be more mothers close by.

"Hey, Jack!" Annie called.

Jack looked up. Annie was at the top of the hill. Feeding magnolia flowers to the giant Anatosaurus!

"She's nice, too, Jack," Annie said.

But suddenly the Anatosaurus made her

39

terrible tuba sound. Annie crouched down and started to chew.

The dinosaur barged down the hill.

She seemed afraid of something.

Jack put the book down on top of his pack. He hurried up to Annie.

"I wonder why she ran away," said Annie. "We were starting to be friends."

Jack looked around. What he saw in the distance almost made him throw up.

An enormous ugly monster was coming across the plain.

He was walking on two big legs. And swinging a long, thick tail. And dangling two tiny arms.

He had a huge head. And his jaws were wide open.

Even from far away Jack could see his long, gleaming teeth.

"Tyrannosaurus rex!" whispered Jack.

42

ENTRY 6

COMPREHENSION PROCESSES
Understand, Evaluate, Create

WRITING TRAITS
Ideas and Content
Word Choice
Conventions—Complete Sentence,
Capital, Period
Presentation

Responding, Making Connections,
Explaining, Generating Ideas

Unit 12 My Book Journal — Use after Exercise 6 and Chapter 6

Entry **6** Chapter 6 **Dinosaur Valley**

(Accept any reasonable response.)
If I were in the land of dinosaurs:

• I would want to ___meet all of the dinosaurs.___
_____

• I would be ___excited to see all of the extinct___
___animals.___

• I ___would take pictures and show all my___
___friends.___

Unit 12 My Book Journal — Use after Exercise 7 and Chapter 7

Entry **7** Chapter 7 **Ready, Set, Go!**

At the end of this chapter, Tyrannosaurus rex was standing between Jack and Annie and the tree house. What do you think will happen next?

First, Jack will _____
_____

Then, the Tyrannosaurus will _____
_____

Finally, I think _____
_____

47

PROCEDURES
For each step, demonstrate and guide practice, as needed. Then have students complete the page independently.

Personal Response: Sentence Completion—Specific Instructions
Have students complete the sentences with personal responses. Encourage students to use snazzy vocabulary words in their writing. Remind them to start sentences with a capital and end with a period. Say something like:

For Entry 6, you are going to write responses to three sentence starters.

Read the first sentence starter in Entry 6. (If I were in the land of dinosaurs, I would want to . . .)

Think about how you might want to complete that sentence.

[Marisa], how would you complete that sentence? (I would want to meet all of the dinosaurs.)
It would be amazing, wouldn't it?

Read the next sentence starter. (I would be . . .)

[Jordyn], how would you complete that sentence? (I would be absolutely thrilled to be in the land of the dinosaurs.)

Wow, [Jordyn], you used the snazzy word *absolutely*. Great job!

Read the last sentence starter. (I . . .)
You can write almost anything here. I can't wait to see what you all come up with.

Self-monitoring
Have students check and correct their work.

COMPREHENSION AND SKILL ACTIVITY 6

★CROSSWORD PUZZLE

COMPREHENSION PROCESSES

Remember, Understand

Identifying—What; Using Vocabulary—
bellow, colony, medallion

PROCEDURES

For each step, demonstrate and guide practice, as needed. Then have students complete the page independently.

Vocabulary: Sentence Completion—Specific Instructions

• Tell students that they will complete a crossword puzzle. Say something like:
Today, you get to do a crossword puzzle. A crossword puzzle has blanks for words that go down the page and across the page.

• Have students read the words in the word bank. Then have students read the sentences and fill in the blanks with words from the bank. Say something like:
Put your finger on the box that says "Word Bank." Read the words. (bellowed, colonies, hunted, medallion, nests)
Now, let's complete each of the sentences with the correct word from the word bank.
Read sentence one. (Jack had found a gold . . . *blank* in the grass.)
Look at the word bank. What did Jack find in the grass? (a medallion)
Read the sentence with the word *medallion* to see if it makes sense.
(Jack had found a gold medallion in the grass.)
Does that make sense? (yes) *Medallion* will be number one in the word puzzle.
Look at the label above the sentence. Now, look at the puzzle.
Will the word go down or across? (down)
This one is done for you. Find it on the puzzle, and cross out the word *medallion* in the word bank.

• Repeat for sentences 2–5, as needed.
• Have students write the correct words in the crossword puzzle.

★ = New in this unit

PASSAGE READING FLUENCY

FLUENCY

Accuracy, Expression, Rate

PROCEDURES

For each step, demonstrate and guide practice, as needed. Then have students complete the page independently.

Passage Reading—Basic Instructions

- Have students read the practice words.
- Have students finger track and whisper read the story two times—the first time for accuracy and the second time for expression. Have students cross out a dinosaur each time they finish.
- Have students do a one-minute Timed Reading and cross out the timer. Say something like:

  You are going to track with your finger and whisper read.

  Read the passage three times. The first time, read for accuracy.

  What will you read for? (accuracy)

  The second time, read for accuracy and expression.

  What will you read for? (accuracy and expression)

  Each time you read, cross out a dinosaur and notice how much better your reading sounds.

  The last time you read, use the timer. Read quickly but accurately and with expression. See if you can finish reading before one minute is up.

> **ACCURACY PRECEDES RATE (Reminder)**
>
> Students should read the story with a high degree of accuracy before proceeding to Timed Readings. Reading for increased rate before establishing a high degree of accuracy may encourage students to guess at words.

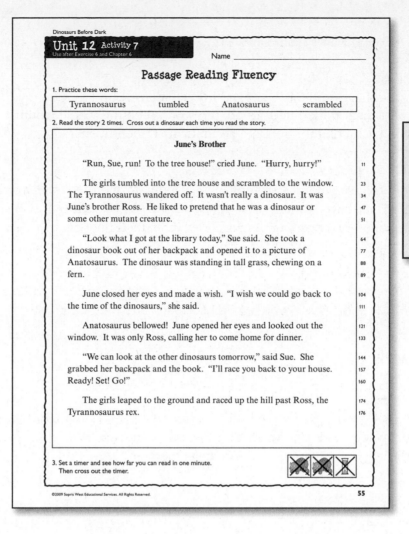

Dinosaurs Before Dark

Unit 12 Activity 7
Use after Exercise 6 and Chapter 6

Name _____

Passage Reading Fluency

1. Practice these words:

Tyrannosaurus	tumbled	Anatosaurus	scrambled

2. Read the story 2 times. Cross out a dinosaur each time you read the story.

June's Brother

"Run, Sue, run! To the tree house!" cried June. "Hurry, hurry!" — 11

The girls tumbled into the tree house and scrambled to the window. — 23
The Tyrannosaurus wandered off. It wasn't really a dinosaur. It was — 34
June's brother Ross. He liked to pretend that he was a dinosaur or — 47
some other mutant creature. — 51

"Look what I got at the library today," Sue said. She took a — 64
dinosaur book out of her backpack and opened it to a picture of — 77
Anatosaurus. The dinosaur was standing in tall grass, chewing on a — 88
fern. — 89

June closed her eyes and made a wish. "I wish we could go back to — 104
the time of the dinosaurs," she said. — 111

Anatosaurus bellowed! June opened her eyes and looked out the — 121
window. It was only Ross, calling her to come home for dinner. — 133

"We can look at the other dinosaurs tomorrow," said Sue. She — 144
grabbed her backpack and the book. "I'll race you back to your house. — 157
Ready! Set! Go!" — 160

The girls leaped to the ground and raced up the hill past Ross, the — 174
Tyrannosaurus rex. — 176

3. Set a timer and see how far you can read in one minute.
   Then cross out the timer.

55

CHECKOUT OPPORTUNITY

Listen to your students read individually while others work. When possible, provide your lowest-performing students with one-to-one practice.

❶ SOUND REVIEW

Use selected Sound Cards from Units 1–12.

❷ SOUND PRACTICE

- For each task, have students spell and say the focus sound in the gray bar. Next, have students read each underlined sound, the word, then the whole column.
- Repeat with each column, building accuracy first, then fluency.

❸ ACCURACY AND FLUENCY BUILDING

- For each task, have students say any underlined part, then read the word.
- Set a pace. Then have students read the whole words in each task and column.
- Provide repeated practice, building accuracy first, then fluency.

D1. Multisyllabic Words

- For the list of words divided by syllables, have students read each syllable, then the whole word. Use the word in a sentence, as appropriate.
- For the list of whole words, build accuracy and then fluency.

valley	The mountains were on both sides of us as we hiked through the . . . *valley.*
monster	An imaginary creature is a . . . *monster.*
bellowing	I want my dog to stop howling and . . . *bellowing.*

E1. Tricky Words

- For each Tricky Word, have students use the sounds and word parts they know to silently sound out the word. Use the word in a sentence to help with pronunciation.
- If the word is unfamiliar, tell students the word.

pushed	Ben put the baby in the stroller and . . . *pushed* . . . it.
where	We were lost and didn't know . . . *where* . . . we were.
nothing	The opposite of everything is . . . *nothing.*

- Have students go back and read the whole words in the column.

❹ WORDS IN CONTEXT

For each word, have students use the sounds and word parts they know to silently sound out the word. Then have students read the sentence. Assist, as needed.

❺ DINOSAUR WORDS

- Have students use the sounds and word parts they know to read each word.
- Use the word in a sentence, as needed.

❻ MORPHOGRAPHS AND AFFIXES

- Have students read the underlined part, then the word.
- Repeat practice with whole words, mixing group and individual turns. Build accuracy, then fluency.

Dinosaurs Before Dark

Unit 12 Exercise 7
Use before Chapter 7

1. **SOUND REVIEW** Use selected Sound Cards from Units 1–12.

2. **SOUND PRACTICE** In each column, have students spell and say the sound, then say any underlined sound and the word. Next, have students read the whole column.

ea as in eagle	**ea** as in bread	**oa**	Bossy <u>E</u>
l<u>ea</u>ped	br<u>ea</u>th	c<u>oa</u>st	r<u>o</u>pe
cl<u>ea</u>r	h<u>ea</u>ds	gr<u>oa</u>ned	r<u>a</u>ced
f<u>ea</u>r	r<u>ea</u>dy	s<u>oa</u>red	n<u>o</u>tebook

3. **ACCURACY AND FLUENCY BUILDING** For each column, have students say any underlined part, then read each word. Next, have students read the whole column.

A1 Mixed Practice	**B1** Word Endings	**C1** Word Endings	**D1** Multisyllabic Words	**E1** Tricky Words
plus	cry	<u>peek</u>ed	val•ley	pushed
<u>f</u>erns	cried	<u>scoop</u>ed	mon•ster	where
<u>y</u>ay	lie	<u>rais</u>ed	bel•low•ing	nothing
belong	lying	<u>dash</u>ed	valley	**E2** Affix Practice
m<u>o</u>ment	hurry	<u>hunch</u>ed	monster	<u>be</u>low
s<u>o</u>und	hurried	<u>glass</u>es	bellowing	<u>be</u>fore
gu<u>a</u>rd		<u>pant</u>ing		<u>be</u>tween
pla<u>ce</u>				

4. **WORDS IN CONTEXT** For each word, have students use the sounds and word parts they know to figure out the word. Then have them read the sentences.

Ⓐ	tu•ba	My brother plays the <u>tuba</u> in the school band.
Ⓑ	ter•ri•ble	When something is very, very bad, it is <u>terrible</u>.
Ⓒ	wan•der•ing	We didn't know where we were going. We were <u>wandering</u>.

5. **DINOSAUR WORDS** Have students use the sounds and word parts they know to figure out the words.

| Tyrannosaurus rex | Pteranodon | Anatosaurus |

6. **MORPHOGRAPHS AND AFFIXES** Have students read the underlined word part, then the word.

| <u>de</u>cide | <u>re</u>charged | thought<u>ful</u> | forgett<u>able</u> | <u>un</u>scrambled |

COMPREHENSION PROCESSES

Understand, Apply

PROCEDURES

Introducing Vocabulary

★ pant ★ panic ★ peer ★ stampede ★ stick close to ★ caught my eye

- For each vocabulary word, have students read the word by parts, then read the whole word.
- Read the student-friendly explanations to students as they follow with their fingers. Then have students use the vocabulary word by following the gray text.
- Review and discuss the illustrations.

  Note: Student vocabulary pages for this unit are found in the students' *Exercise Book 2*.

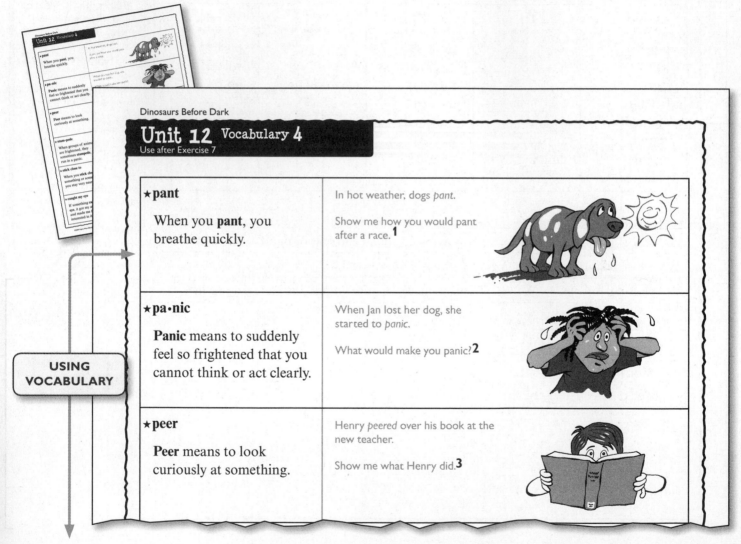

Dinosaurs Before Dark

Unit 12 Vocabulary 4
Use after Exercise 7

USING VOCABULARY

★pant When you **pant**, you breathe quickly.	In hot weather, dogs *pant*. Show me how you would pant after a race. **1**
★pa·nic **Panic** means to suddenly feel so frightened that you cannot think or act clearly.	When Jan lost her dog, she started to *panic*. What would make you panic? **2**
★peer **Peer** means to look curiously at something.	Henry *peered* over his book at the new teacher. Show me what Henry did. **3**

❶ **Apply:** Demonstrating; Using Vocabulary—pant

❷ **Apply:** Using Vocabulary—panic (I panic when I have to talk in front of the whole class. I panic when I miss the bus.)

❸ **Apply:** Demonstrating; Using Vocabulary—peer (He looked at the new teacher.)

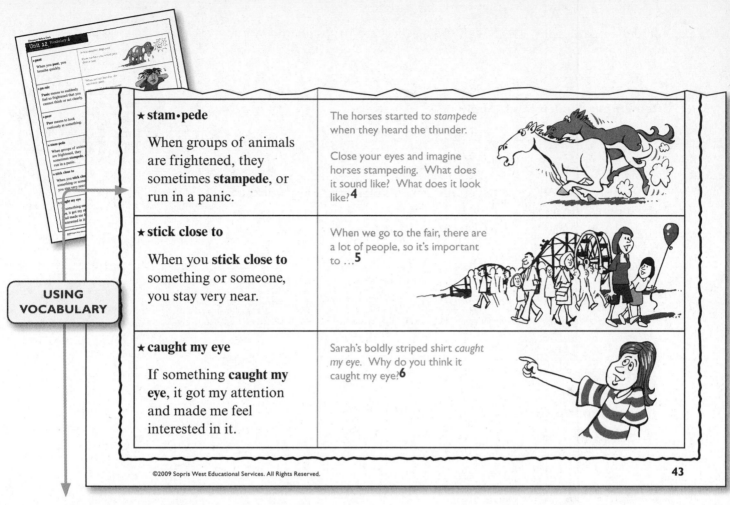

USING VOCABULARY

★ **stam•pede** When groups of animals are frightened, they sometimes **stampede**, or run in a panic.	The horses started to *stampede* when they heard the thunder. Close your eyes and imagine horses stampeding. What does it sound like? What does it look like?**4**
★ **stick close to** When you **stick close to** something or someone, you stay very near.	When we go to the fair, there are a lot of people, so it's important to …**5**
★ **caught my eye** If something **caught my eye**, it got my attention and made me feel interested in it.	Sarah's boldly striped shirt *caught my eye*. Why do you think it caught my eye?**6**

43

❹ **Understand:** Visualizing, Describing; **Apply:** Using Vocabulary—stampede (A stampede would be very loud, like thunder. The horses would run fast, with their manes flying in the wind.)

❺ **Apply:** Using Idioms and Expressions—stick close to (stick close to each other)

❻ **Apply:** Demonstrating; Using Idioms and Expressions—caught my eye (It was bold and striped and got my attention.)

USING VOCABULARY

Be enthusiastic about learning new words. Keep a running list of words you would like to use and encourage students to use. Keep the list handy when you are teaching. Put students' names on the board to acknowledge use of a word.
Say things like:
Wow! [Karine] used the expression *caught my eye* when she asked if she could borrow my book.

CHAPTER 7 INSTRUCTIONS
Students read pages 43–45 with the teacher and pages 46 and 47 on their own.

COMPREHENSION PROCESSES
Remember, Understand, Apply

PROCEDURES

1. **Reviewing Chapter 6**

   Identifying—What, Where; Inferring; Explaining; Using Vocabulary—colonies, suspense
   You read the last part of Chapter 6 on your own. Let's review what you found out.
   What did Jack read about the duck-billed dinosaurs? (They lived in colonies. A few mothers babysat.)
   Where were the other mother dinosaurs? (They were looking for food.)
   The book doesn't tell, but what do you think it means when the dinosaur makes the tuba sound? (It's frightened. It's warning others.)
   At the end of the chapter, the author builds suspense. What does Jack see? (He sees a T. rex.)

2. **Introducing Chapter 7**

   Identifying—Title
   What's the title of the chapter? (Ready, Set, Go!)

3. **First Reading**
   • Ask questions and discuss the story as indicated by the blue text in this teacher's guide.
   • Mix group and individual turns, independent of your voice.
     Have students work toward a group accuracy goal of 0–3 errors.
     Quietly keep track of errors made by all students in the group.
   • After reading the story, practice any difficult words.
     Reread the story if students have not reached the accuracy goal.

4. **Second Reading, Short Passage Practice: Developing Prosody**
   • Demonstrate expressive, fluent reading of the first paragraph.
     Read at a rate slightly faster than the students' rate.
   • Guide practice with your voice.
   • Provide individual turns while others track with their fingers and whisper read.
   • Repeat with one paragraph or page at a time. Repeat steps with each remaining paragraph.

> **CORRECTING DECODING ERRORS**
>
> During story reading, gently correct any error, then have students reread the sentence.

7
Ready, Set, Go!

"Run, Annie! Run!" cried Jack. "To the tree house!"

They dashed down the hill together. Through the tall grass, through the ferns, past the Pteranodon, and right to the rope ladder.

They scrambled up. Seconds later they tumbled into the tree house.

Annie leaped to the window.

"He's going away!" she said, panting.

Jack pushed his glasses into place. He looked through the window with her.

43

The Tyrannosaurus was wandering off.

But then the monster stopped and turned around.

"Duck!" said Jack.

The two of them hunched down.

After a long moment, they raised their heads. They peeked out again.

"Coast clear," said Jack.

"Yay," whispered Annie.

"We have to get out of here," said Jack.

"You made a wish before," said Annie.

"I wish we could go back to Frog Creek," said Jack.

Nothing happened.

"I wish—"

"Wait. You were looking at a picture in the dinosaur book. Remember?"

The dinosaur book.

Jack groaned. "Oh, no. I left the book and

44

After Reading Page 43

❶ Apply: Inferring, Explaining
Jack and Annie did not run away from the Pteranodon, the Triceratops, or the duck-billed dinosaur. Why do you think they are running now?
(The Tyrannosaurus rex is a meat eater. It's dangerous. It has big teeth.)

After Reading Page 44

❶ Remember: Identifying—What
What did Jack wish for?
(He wished to go home.)

❷ Remember: Identifying—What
What happened when he wished to go home?
(Nothing happened.)

❸ Apply: Inferring, Explaining—Problem
Jack left the dinosaur book on the hill. The book doesn't tell you, but why is that a problem?
(The book is what took them to the land of the dinosaurs. They may need the book to get back home.)

my pack on the hill. I have to go back."

"Oh, forget it," said Annie.

"I can't," said Jack. "The book doesn't belong to us. Plus my notebook's in my pack. With all my notes."

"Hurry!" said Annie.

Jack hurried down the rope ladder.

He leaped to the ground.

He raced past the Pteranodon, through the ferns, through the tall grass, and up the hill.

He looked down.

There was his pack, lying on the ground. On top of it was the dinosaur book.

But now the valley below was filled with Anatosauruses. All standing guard around the nests.

Where had they been? Did fear of the Tyrannosaurus send them home?

Jack took a deep breath.

45

After Reading Page 45

❶ **Apply:** Predicting
What do you think is going to happen next?

CHAPTER 7 INSTRUCTIONS

Students read pages 46 and 47 without the teacher, independently or with partners.

COMPREHENSION PROCESSES

Understand, Apply

PREP NOTE

Setting a Purpose

Write questions on a chalkboard, white board, or large piece of paper before working with your small group.

PROCEDURES FOR READING ON YOUR OWN

1. **Getting Ready**

   Have students turn to page 46.

2. **Setting a Purpose**

   Inferring; Explaining—Problem

   Before students begin reading, say something like:
   As you read the rest of the chapter, try to answer the following questions. When you are done, stop and think about the questions with your partner.
   - Why is Chapter 7 titled "Ready, Set, Go!"?
   - At the end of the chapter, the author builds suspense. What was Jack's problem?

3. **Reading on Your Own: Partner or Whisper Reading**
   - Have students take turns reading the page with a partner or have students whisper read pages 46–47 on their own.
   - Continue having students track each word with their fingers.

4. **Comprehension and Skill Work**

   Tell students that they will work on their Book Journal and do Comprehension and Skill Activity 8 after they read on their own. Guide practice, as needed. For teacher directions, see pages 99 and 100.

5. **Homework 7: New Passage**

Ready! Set! Go!

He charged down the hill. He leaped to his backpack. He scooped it up. He grabbed the dinosaur book.

A terrible tuba sound! Another! Another! All the Anatosauruses were bellowing at him.

Jack took off.

He raced up to the hilltop.

He started down the hill.

He stopped.

The Tyrannosaurus rex was back! And he was standing between Jack and the tree house!

ENTRY 7

COMPREHENSION PROCESSES

Apply, Create

WRITING TRAITS

Ideas and Content
Organization—Sequencing
Word Choice
Conventions—Complete Sentence,
Capital, Period
Presentation

Using Vocabulary—suspense; Predicting
Explaining; Generating Ideas

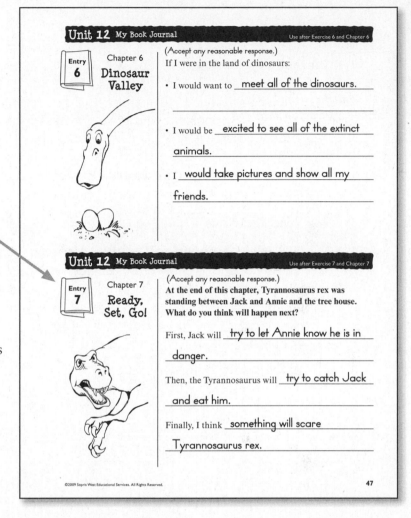

PROCEDURES

For each step, demonstrate and guide practice, as needed. Then have students complete the page independently.

Personal Response: Sentence Completion—Specific Instructions
Have students complete the sentences with personal predictions. Encourage students to use snazzy vocabulary words in their writing. Remind them to start sentences with a capital and end with a period. Say something like:
The end of Chapter 7 left us in suspense. How did the author leave us in suspense?
(We don't know what the Tyrannosaurus Rex is going to do.)

Read the top of Entry 7.
(At the end of this chapter, Tyrannosaurus rex was standing between Jack and Annie and the tree house. What do you think will happen next?)
I know you are wondering what will happen next. I can't wait to read your personal predictions.

The sentences have been started for you. Read the first sentence starter. (First, Jack will . . .)
What do you think Jack will do?

Model or, if time allows, have partners discuss what they might write. Say something like:
Partner 1, tell your partner what you think might happen.
After about a minute say: Partner 2, your turn.
After about a minute say: Let's share your predictions.
(First, Jack will hesitate, and the Tyrannosaurus will spot him.)

Self-monitoring
Have students check and correct their work.

MAIN IDEA AND SUPPORTING DETAILS

COMPREHENSION PROCESSES
Remember, Apply

WRITING TRAITS
Conventions—Period

PROCEDURES

For each step, demonstrate and guide practice, as needed. Then have students complete the page independently.

1. **Topic: Answering Questions—Basic Instructions** (Item 1)
   - Have students read the paragraph in the box.
   - Have students read the question and write the topic in the blank.

2. **Main Idea/Supporting Details: Hierarchy Chart—Basic Instructions** (Item 2)
   - Have students complete the graphic organizer by listing supporting details.
   - Have students select and complete the main idea sentence.
   - Remind students to use a period at the end of the sentence.

Identifying—Topic

Using Graphic
Organizer
Identifying—
Supporting Details
Inferring—
Main Idea; Sentence
Completion

Dinosaurs Before Dark

Unit 12 Activity 8
Use after Exercise 7 and Chapter 7

Name _____

Main Idea and Supporting Details

Tyrannosaurus rex was a dangerous dinosaur. It was 40 feet long and weighed seven tons. It had a mouthful of sharp teeth that were six inches long. Tyrannosaurus rex was a meat eater with very strong jaws. All the other dinosaurs had to watch out or they would become a T. rex meal.

1 **What is this paragraph about?**

Tyrannosaurus rex

2 **Supporting Details**

List details.

- 40 feet long and
  weighed seven tons

- a mouthful of
  sharp teeth

- a meat eater with
  strong jaws

Main Idea:

Tyrannosaurus rex was

a dangerous dinosaur.

○ a big dinosaur
● a dangerous dinosaur
○ a hungry dinosaur

56

CHECKOUT OPPORTUNITY

Listen to your students read individually while others work. When possible, provide your lowest-performing students with one-to-one practice.

❶ SOUND REVIEW

Have students read the sounds and key word phrases in each row. Work for accuracy, then fluency.

❷ SHIFTY WORD BLENDING

For each word, have students say the underlined sound. Then have them sound out the word smoothly and say it. Use the words in sentences, as appropriate.

❸ ACCURACY AND FLUENCY BUILDING

- For each task, have students say any underlined part, then read the word.
- Set a pace. Then have students read the whole words in each task and column.
- Provide repeated practice, building accuracy first, then fluency.

C1. Related Words

- For each set, tell students the related word. Then have them read the words in the set. Say something like:
  All the words in this group are related to the word *close*. Read the words.
- Repeat for "open."

E1. Tricky Words

- For each Tricky Word, have students use the sounds and word parts they know to silently sound out the word. Use the word in a sentence to help with pronunciation.
- If the word is unfamiliar, tell students the word.

heart	Can you hear the beating of my . . . *heart?*
steak	For dinner I had a delicious beef . . . *steak.*
wandered	Where had the little lost sheep . . . *wandered?*
caught	The robber didn't want to get . . . *caught.*
climb	Our cat likes to . . . *climb.*
straight	One of our class rules is to sit up . . . *straight.*
magnolia	There were beautiful blossoms on the . . . *magnolia* . . . tree.

- Have students go back and read the whole words in the column.

❹ MULTISYLLABIC WORDS

For each word, have students read the syllables, then the whole word. Use the word in a sentence, as appropriate.

human	Every man, woman, and child is a . . . *human.*
horrible	Watching the house burn down was . . . *horrible.*
direction	I am lost. Tell me which . . . *direction* . . . to go.
information	I asked a question so I could get more . . . *information.*
stampede	When the cows are frightened, they sometimes . . . *stampede.*
overhead	A bird flew . . . *overhead.*

❺ MORPHOGRAPHS AND AFFIXES

- Have students read the underlined part, then the word.
- Repeat practice with whole words, mixing group and individual turns. Build accuracy, then fluency.

Dinosaurs Before Dark

Unit 12 Exercise 8
Use before Chapter 8

1. SOUND REVIEW Have students review sounds for accuracy, then for fluency.

Ⓐ	eu as in blue	ow as in snow	-y as in fly	a as in ago	ch as in chicken
Ⓑ	e_u	oi	i_e	or	ir

2. SHIFTY WORD BLENDING For each word, have students say the underlined part, sound out smoothly, then read the word.

l<u>igh</u>t	m<u>igh</u>t	m<u>ea</u>t	<u>ch</u>eat	<u>ch</u>art

3. ACCURACY AND FLUENCY BUILDING For each column, have students say any underlined part, then read each word. Next, have students read the whole column.

A1 Mixed Practice	B1 Bossy <u>E</u>	C1 Related Words	D1 Word Endings	E1 Tricky Words
l<u>ea</u>ve	h<u>i</u>de	close	<u>peer</u>ed	heart
h<u>o</u>p	al<u>i</u>ve	closer	<u>peek</u>ed	steak
j<u>aw</u>s	kn<u>i</u>ves	closing	<u>point</u>ed	wandered
sk<u>y</u>			<u>roar</u>ed	caught
spr<u>ea</u>d	sh<u>a</u>ke	open	<u>sail</u>ed	climb
<u>kn</u>ow	sh<u>a</u>king	opening	<u>beat</u>ing	straight
shad<u>ow</u>		opened	<u>large</u>st	magnolia
	gl<u>i</u>de	unopened	<u>flap</u>ping	
	gl<u>i</u>ding			

4. MULTISYLLABIC WORDS Have students read each word part, then read each whole word.

Ⓐ	hu·man	human	hor·ri·ble	horrible
Ⓑ	di·rec·tion	direction	in·for·ma·tion	information
Ⓒ	stam·pede	stampede	o·ver·head	overhead

5. MORPHOGRAPHS AND AFFIXES Have students read the underlined word part, then the word.

Ⓐ	hard<u>ly</u>	forget<u>ful</u>	comfort<u>able</u>
Ⓑ	<u>ex</u>plain	<u>bi</u>monthly	<u>de</u>termine

> **ENCOURAGING DESIRED BEHAVIORS**
> **(Reminder)**
>
> Make a special effort to notice and congratulate the least mature students whenever they are taking steps toward greater cooperation, responsibility, and independence.

CHAPTER 8 INSTRUCTIONS

Students read pages 48 and 49 with the teacher and pages 50–53 on their own.

COMPREHENSION PROCESSES

Remember, Understand, Apply

PROCEDURES

1. **Reviewing Chapter 7**

   Inferring; Explaining—Problem

   Let's review what you found out in Chapter 7.

   Why is Chapter 7 titled "Ready, Set, Go!" (Jack needed to grab his backpack and the book, but he knew the Tyrannosaurus rex was around. He told himself "ready, set, go" to work up the courage to run and get his things.)

   What was Jack's problem? (The Tyrannosaurus rex was right between Jack and the safety of the tree house.)

2. **Introducing Chapter 8**

   Identifying—Title; Predicting

   What's the title of the chapter? (A Giant Shadow)

   Jack has a problem. What do you think is going to happen in this chapter?

3. **First Reading**

   • Ask questions and discuss the story as indicated by the blue text in this teacher's guide.

   • Mix group and individual turns, independent of your voice.
   Have students work toward a group accuracy goal of 0–2 errors.
   Quietly keep track of errors made by all students in the group.

   • After reading the story, practice any difficult words. Reread the story if students have not reached the accuracy goal.

4. **Second Reading, Timed Readings: Repeated Reading**

   • As time allows, have students do Timed Readings while others follow along.

   • Time individuals for 30 seconds and encourage each child to work for a personal best.

   • Determine words correct per minute. Record student scores.

8

A Giant Shadow

Jack jumped behind the magnolia tree.

His heart was beating so fast he could hardly think.

He peeked out at the giant monster. The horrible-looking creature was opening and closing his huge jaws. His teeth were as big as steak knives.

Don't panic. Think.

Jack peered down at the valley.

Good. The duck-billed dinosaurs were sticking close to their nests.

48

Jack looked back at the Tyrannosaurus.

Good. The monster still didn't seem to know he was there.

Don't panic. Think. *Think.* Maybe there's information in the book.

Jack opened the dinosaur book. He found Tyrannosaurus rex. He read:

Tyrannosaurus rex was the largest meat-eating land animal of all time. If it were alive today, it would eat a human in one bite.

Great. The book was no help at all.

Okay. He couldn't hide on the other side of the hill. The Anatosauruses might stampede.

Okay. He couldn't run to the tree house. The Tyrannosaurus might run faster.

Okay. Maybe he should just wait. Wait for the monster to leave.

49

After Reading Page 48

❶ Understand: Describing—Problem
Describe Jack's problem.
(A Tyrannosaurus rex is between him and the tree house.)

❷ Remember: Identifying—What
At the beginning of this chapter, what is Jack doing?
(He's hiding behind a tree.)

❸ Apply: Inferring; Explaining; Using Vocabulary—panic
Jack told himself, "Don't panic." Why do you think he said that?
(He was scared, but he wanted to stay calm and think clearly about what to do.)

After Reading Page 49

❶ Understand: Explaining—Solution
What did Jack do to try to solve his problem?
(He read about T. rex in the book.)

❷ Remember: Identifying—What
What did the book say?
(Tyrannosaurus rex was the largest meat-eating animal. It could eat a human.)

❸ Apply: Inferring
Did the book help Jack solve his problem?
(No, it probably made him more scared.)

CHAPTER 8 INSTRUCTIONS

Students read pages 50–53 without the teacher, independently or with partners.

COMPREHENSION PROCESSES

Remember, Understand, Apply

PREP NOTE

Setting a Purpose

Write questions on a chalkboard, white board, or large piece of paper before working with your small group.

PROCEDURES

1. Getting Ready

Have students turn to page 50.

2. Setting a Purpose

Inferring; Explaining; Identifying—What; Predicting; Using Vocabulary— suspense

Before beginning reading, say something like:
As you read the rest of the chapter, try to answer the following questions. When you are done, stop and think about the questions with your partner.

• Why did Jack think Annie was nuts?

• What did the author do to build suspense at the end of Chapter 8?

• Do you think Jack will be saved?

3. Reading on Your Own: Partner or Whisper Reading

• Have students take turns reading every other page with a partner, or have students whisper read pages 50–53 on their own.

• Continue having students track each word with their fingers.

4. Comprehension and Skill Work

Tell students that they will work on their Book Journal and do Comprehension and Skill Activity 9 after they read on their own. Guide practice, as needed. For teacher directions, see pages 109 and 110.

5. Homework 8: New Passage

Jack peeked around the tree.

The Tyrannosaurus had wandered *closer* to the hill.

50

Something caught Jack's eye. Annie was coming down the rope ladder!

Was she nuts? What was she doing?

51

Jack watched Annie hop off the ladder.

She went straight to the Pteranodon. She was talking to him. She was flapping her arms. She pointed at Jack, at the sky, at the tree house.

She *was* nuts!

"Go! Go back up the tree!" Jack whispered. "Go!"

Suddenly Jack heard a roar.

The Tyrannosaurus rex was looking in his direction.

Jack hit the ground.

The Tyrannosaurus rex was coming toward the hill.

Jack felt the ground shaking.

Should he run? Crawl back into Dinosaur Valley? Climb the magnolia tree?

Just then a giant shadow covered Jack. He looked up.

52

The Pteranodon was gliding overhead. The giant creature sailed down toward the top of the hill.

He was coming straight for Jack.

53

ENTRY 8

COMPREHENSION PROCESSES

Apply, Evaluate, Create

WRITING TRAITS

Ideas and Content
Word Choice
Conventions—Complete Sentence,
Capital, Period
Presentation

> Responding; Explaining; Sentence
> Completion; Generating Ideas
> Using Vocabulary—panic

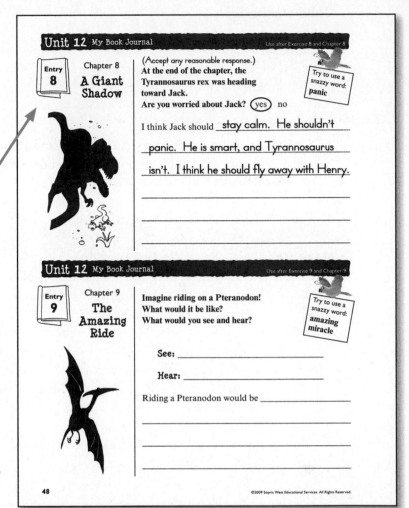

PROCEDURES

For each step, demonstrate and guide
practice, as needed. Then have students
complete the page independently.

Personal Response: Paragraph
Writing—Specific Instructions

Have students complete the sentence
with a personal response. Encourage
students to use the snazzy word "panic"
in their writing. Remind them to start
sentences with a capital and end with
a period.

This was an exciting chapter. Read the sentences for Entry 8.

(At the end of the chapter, the Tyrannosaurus rex was heading toward Jack.
Are you worried about Jack?)

Thumbs up if you are going to circle "yes."

Thumbs down if you going to circle "no."

Read the sentence starter for the next part. (I think Jack should . . .)

What do you think Jack should do? [Ryan], what do you think?

(He should not panic and just stay still. The Tyrannosaurus rex may not see him.)

Excellent, Ryan, you used that snazzy word *panic*.

I know you all have lots of ideas about what Jack should do. You will get to write your own response
in your journal.

Remember four things. Use your best handwriting so you can be proud of your work. Try to use the
snazzy word *panic*. Remember to start your sentences with a capital and end them with a period or
exclamation mark. Remember to use a capital at the beginning of anyone's name.

Self-monitoring

Have students check and correct their work.

STORY COMPREHENSION AND MAZE READING

COMPREHENSION PROCESSES

Understand, Apply

PROCEDURES

For each step, demonstrate and guide practice, as needed. Then have students complete the page independently.

Story Comprehension

1. **Selection Response—Basic Instructions** (Items 1–3)

    Have students read the sentence or question and fill in the bubble and/or blanks, or check the blanks with the correct answers.

2. **True/False: Selection Response** (Items 4, 5)

Maze Reading—Specific Instructions

- Tell students that the paragraph in the box is about the Tyrannosaurus rex.
- Review directions for completing a Maze Reading. Say something like:

  Remember, a maze is like a puzzle.

  You will choose the correct words to complete the sentences.

  Read and stop at the parentheses.

  (Tyrannosaurus was a very dangerous animal. This dinosaur was a meat . . .)

  There are three choices. Try reading the whole sentence with the first word choice.

  (This dinosaur was a meat . . . *easy*.) Does meat *easy* make sense? (no)

  No. That is not correct. So, what should you do? (Try the next word.)

  Read the sentence with the next word. (This dinosaur was a meat . . . *eater*.)

  Does that make sense? (yes)

  Let's try the last word to make sure that it is not the one we want to choose.

  (This dinosaur was a meat . . . *runner*.) Does that make sense? (no)

  The word that makes sense is the word *eater*, so circle the word *eater*.

- Have students complete the remainder of the paragraph.
- Tell students to reread the paragraph to make sure it makes sense.

COMPREHENSION AND SKILL ACTIVITY 9

Using Vocabulary—suspense

Inferring

Identifying—Action Inferring

Comprehension Monitoring, Test Taking

Comprehension Monitoring, Test Taking

Comprehension Monitoring, Test Taking

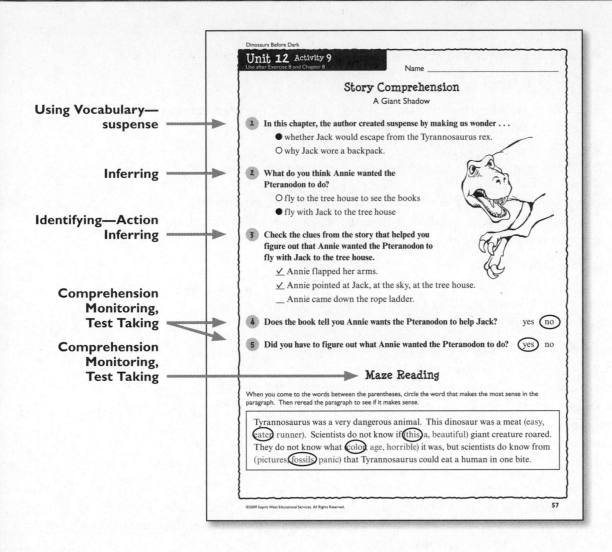

Dinosaurs Before Dark

Unit 12 Activity 9
Use after Exercise 8 and Chapter 8

Name _____

Story Comprehension
A Giant Shadow

1. In this chapter, the author created suspense by making us wonder . . .
   - ● whether Jack would escape from the Tyrannosaurus rex.
   - ○ why Jack wore a backpack.

2. What do you think Annie wanted the Pteranodon to do?
   - ○ fly to the tree house to see the books
   - ● fly with Jack to the tree house

3. Check the clues from the story that helped you figure out that Annie wanted the Pteranodon to fly with Jack to the tree house.
   - ✓ Annie flapped her arms.
   - ✓ Annie pointed at Jack, at the sky, at the tree house.
   - ___ Annie came down the rope ladder.

4. Does the book tell you Annie wants the Pteranodon to help Jack?   yes   (no)

5. Did you have to figure out what Annie wanted the Pteranodon to do?   (yes)   no

Maze Reading

When you come to the words between the parentheses, circle the word that makes the most sense in the paragraph. Then reread the paragraph to see if it makes sense.

Tyrannosaurus was a very dangerous animal. This dinosaur was a meat (easy, **eater**, runner). Scientists do not know if (**this**, a, beautiful) giant creature roared. They do not know what (**color**, age, horrible) it was, but scientists do know from (pictures, **fossils**, panic) that Tyrannosaurus could eat a human in one bite.

57

❶ SOUND REVIEW

Have students read the sounds and key word phrases. Work for accuracy, then fluency.

❷ SOUND PRACTICE

- For each task, have students spell and say the focus sound in the gray bar. Next, have students read each underlined sound, the word, then the whole column.
- Repeat with each column, building accuracy first, then fluency.

❸ ACCURACY AND FLUENCY BUILDING

- For each task, have students say any underlined part, then read the word.
- Set a pace. Then have students read the whole words in each task and column.
- Provide repeated practice, building accuracy first, then fluency.

C1. Multisyllabic Words

- For the list of words divided by syllables, have students read each syllable, then the whole word. Use the word in a sentence, as appropriate.
- For the list of whole words, build accuracy and then fluency.

teetered	The circus performer . . . *teetered* . . . on the tightrope.
dizzy	Spinning around in circles makes me . . . *dizzy.*
photograph	Smile when someone takes your . . . *photograph.*
wobbly	The baby horse tried to walk, but its legs were . . . *wobbly.*
forward	The opposite of backward is . . . *forward.*
reptiles	Turtles are . . . *reptiles.*
whistling	When the dogs didn't come, Jack started . . . *whistling* . . . for them.

D1. Tricky Words

- For each Tricky Word, have students use the sounds and word parts they know to silently sound out the word. Use the word in a sentence to help with pronunciation.
- If the word is unfamiliar, tell students the word.

miracle	A wonderful thing that happens that seems impossible is called a . . . *miracle.*
though	Tammy didn't mean it, even . . . *though* . . . she said it.
toward	We saw the house in the distance. We walked . . . *toward* . . . it.
believe	The story was so silly that Amy knew not to . . . *believe* . . . it.
climb	Sam wishes he had a big tree in his yard so he could . . . *climb* . . . it.

- Have students go back and read the whole words in the column.

❹ WORDS IN CONTEXT

For each word, have students use the sounds and word parts they know to silently sound out the word. Then have students read the sentence. Assist, as needed.

❺ MORPHOGRAPHS AND AFFIXES

- Have students read the underlined part, then the word.
- Repeat practice with whole words, mixing group and individual turns. Build accuracy, then fluency.

Dinosaurs Before Dark

Unit 12 Exercise 9
Use before Chapter 9

1. SOUND REVIEW Have students review sounds for accuracy, then for fluency.

A	-y as in baby	OW as in cow	O as in open	i as in pilot	a_e as in cake
B	gi	all	au	ph	o_e

2. SOUND PRACTICE In each column, have students spell and say the sound, then say any underlined sound and the word. Next, have students read the whole column.

ea as in bread	ea as in eagle	oa	a as in ago	igh
heavy	leaf	soared	amazing	bright
feather	eased	coasted	alert	sunlight
heading	screamed	moan	aside	tightly

3. ACCURACY AND FLUENCY BUILDING For each column, have students say any underlined part, then read each word. Next, have students read the whole column.

A1 Mixed Practice	B1 Word Endings	C1 Multisyllabic Words		D1 Tricky Words
spun	steady	tee•tered	teetered	miracle
bolted	steadied	diz•zy	dizzy	though
slid		pho•to•graph	photograph	toward
chomping	graze	wob•bly	wobbly	believe
fault	grazing	for•ward	forward	climb
circled	ride	rep•tile	reptile	
	riding	whis•tling	whistling	

4. WORDS IN CONTEXT For each word, have students use the sounds and word parts they know to figure out the word. Then have them read the sentence.

A	bush•es	The roses on the bushes smelled very sweet.
B	a•gainst	He sailed his boat against the wind, straight up the river.
C	Penn•syl•va•nia	I was supposed to go to Pennsylvania for the summer.

5. MORPHOGRAPHS AND AFFIXES Have students read each underlined part, then the word.

began	restarted	unscrambled	absolutely

45

113

COMPREHENSION PROCESSES

Understand, Apply

PROCEDURES

Introducing Vocabulary

> ★teeter ★miracle ★clasp ★engraving ★steady yourself

- For each vocabulary word, have students read the word by parts, then read the whole word.
- Read the student-friendly explanations to students as they follow with their fingers. Then have students use the vocabulary word by following the gray text.
- Review and discuss the illustrations.
  Note: Student vocabulary pages for this unit are found in the students' *Exercise Book 2*.

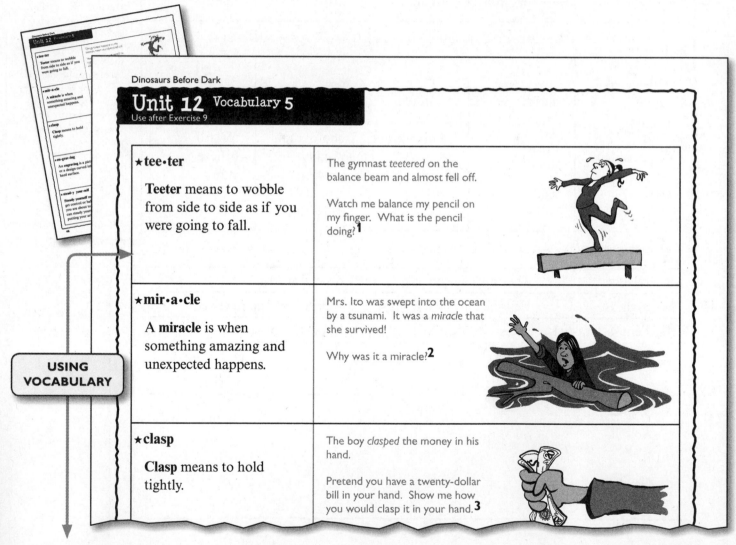

Dinosaurs Before Dark

Unit 12 Vocabulary 5
Use after Exercise 9

USING VOCABULARY

★tee·ter	The gymnast *teetered* on the balance beam and almost fell off.
Teeter means to wobble from side to side as if you were going to fall.	Watch me balance my pencil on my finger. What is the pencil doing?**1**
★mir·a·cle	Mrs. Ito was swept into the ocean by a tsunami. It was a *miracle* that she survived!
A **miracle** is when something amazing and unexpected happens.	Why was it a miracle?**2**
★clasp	The boy *clasped* the money in his hand.
Clasp means to hold tightly.	Pretend you have a twenty-dollar bill in your hand. Show me how you would clasp it in your hand.**3**

❶ **Apply:** Using Vocabulary—teeter (The pencil is teetering.)

❷ **Apply:** Using Vocabulary—miracle (A tsunami is big and powerful. It is amazing that someone could live through it.)

❸ **Apply:** Demonstrating; Using Vocabulary—clasp

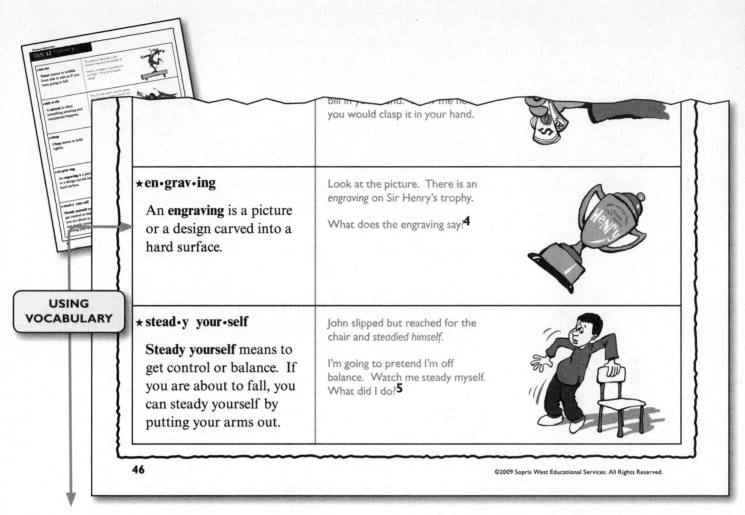

USING VOCABULARY

★**en•grav•ing**

An **engraving** is a picture or a design carved into a hard surface.

Look at the picture. There is an *engraving* on Sir Henry's trophy.

What does the engraving say?**4**

★**stead•y your•self**

Steady yourself means to get control or balance. If you are about to fall, you can steady yourself by putting your arms out.

John slipped but reached for the chair and *steadied himself*.

I'm going to pretend I'm off balance. Watch me steady myself. What did I do?**5**

46

❹ **Apply:** Using Vocabulary—engraving (Henry)

❺ **Apply:** Using Idioms and Expressions—steady yourself (You steadied yourself.)

USING VOCABULARY

Be enthusiastic about learning new words. Keep a running list of words you would like to use and encourage students to use. Keep the list handy when you are teaching. Put students' names on the board to acknowledge use of a word.
Say things like:
[Katie] used the word *clasp* when she talked about carrying the book bag. What a great way to use a vocabulary word!

CHAPTER 9 INSTRUCTIONS

Students read pages 54–57 with the teacher and pages 58–60 on their own.

COMPREHENSION PROCESSES

Remember, Understand, Apply

PROCEDURES

1. Reviewing Chapter 8

Inferring; Explaining; Identifying—What; Predicting; Using Vocabulary—suspense

Let's review what you found out by the end of Chapter 8.

Why did Jack think Annie was nuts?

(Annie was talking to the Pteranodon and flapping her arms.
She should have stayed in the tree where she was safe.)

What did the author do to build suspense at the end of Chapter 8?

(Jack saw the Pteranodon flying over his head.)

Do you think Jack will be saved? (Yes. He's a main character!)

2. Introducing Chapter 9

Identifying—Title; Predicting

What's the title? (The Amazing Ride)

What do you think is going to happen next?

3. First Reading

- Ask questions and discuss the story as indicated by the blue text in this teacher's guide.
- Mix group and individual turns, independent of your voice.
  Have students work toward a group accuracy goal of 0–3 errors.
  Quietly keep track of errors made by all students in the group.
- After reading the story, practice any difficult words.
  Reread the story if students have not reached the accuracy goal.

4. Second Reading, Short Passage Practice: Developing Prosody

- Demonstrate expressive, fluent reading of the first two paragraphs.
- Guide practice with your voice.
- Provide individual turns while others track with their fingers and whisper read.
- Repeat with one paragraph or page at a time.

> **CORRECTING DECODING ERRORS**
> During story reading, gently correct any error, then have students reread the sentence.

9

The Amazing Ride

The Pteranodon coasted down to the ground.

He stared at Jack with his bright, alert eyes.

What was Jack supposed to do? Climb on? "But I'm too heavy," thought Jack.

Don't think. Just do it.

Jack looked at the Tyrannosaurus.

He was starting up the hill. His giant teeth were flashing in the sunlight.

Okay. Don't think. Just do it!

Jack put his book in his pack. Then he eased down onto the Pteranodon's back.

54

He held on tightly.

The creature moved forward. He spread out his wings—and lifted off the ground!

They teetered this way. Then that.

Jack nearly fell off.

The Pteranodon steadied himself, then rose into the sky.

Jack looked down. The Tyrannosaurus was chomping the air and staring up at him.

The Pteranodon glided away.

He sailed over the hilltop.

He circled over the valley. Over all the nests filled with babies. Over all the giant duck-billed dinosaurs.

Then the Pteranodon soared out over the plain—over the Triceratops who was grazing in the high grass.

It was amazing! It was a miracle!

Jack felt like a bird. As light as a feather.

55

After Reading Page 54

❶ **Understand:** Defining and Using Vocabulary—hesitate
Jack hesitated before he climbed onto the Pteranodon. What does hesitate mean?
(Hesitate means to pause because you're not sure. Jack waited for a moment . . .)

❷ **Apply:** Inferring, Explaining
Why did Jack pause for a moment?
(He was afraid he was too heavy for the Pteranodon to carry.)

After Reading Page 55

❶ **Apply:** Demonstrating; Understand: Defining Vocabulary—teeter
The book said Jack and the Pteranodon teetered this way and that. Show me with your hand how they teetered.

❷ **Understand:** Explaining; Using Vocabulary—amazing, miracle
What was the *miracle*?
(Jack was flying through the sky. He was taking an amazing ride on a Pteranodon.)

❸ **Understand:** Describing
Describe what Jack saw.
(Jack saw the valley with the dinosaur nests, the giant duck-billed dinosaurs, Triceratops grazing in the grass . . .)

The wind was rushing through his hair. The air smelled sweet and fresh.

He whooped. He laughed.

Jack couldn't believe it. He was riding on the back of an ancient flying reptile!

After Reading Page 56

❶ **Understand:** Defining and Using Vocabulary—ancient
The book says that Jack was riding on an ancient flying reptile. What does ancient mean?
(Ancient means very, very old, maybe millions of years old.)

❷ **Apply:** Viewing, Inferring
Look at the picture. How do you think Jack feels?
(Jack must be very excited!)

CHAPTER 9 INSTRUCTIONS

Students read pages 58–60 without the teacher, independently or with partners.

COMPREHENSION PROCESSES

Remember, Understand

PREP NOTE
Setting a Purpose
Write questions on a chalkboard, white board, or large piece of paper before working with your small group.

PROCEDURES FOR READING ON YOUR OWN

1. Getting Ready

Have students turn to page 58.

2. Setting a Purpose

Explaining; Identifying—What

Before beginning reading, say something like:

As you read the rest of the chapter, try to answer the following questions. When you are done, stop and think about the questions with your partner.

- What happened to the Pteranodon?
- What happened to the Tyrannosaurus?
- What happened to Jack and Annie?
- At the end of the chapter, what did Jack and Annie wish for?

3. Reading on Your Own: Partner or Whisper Reading

- Have students take turns reading every other page with a partner, or have students whisper read pages 58–60 on their own.
- Continue having students track each word with their fingers.

4. Comprehension and Skill Work

Tell students that they will work on their Book Journal and do Comprehension and Skill Activity 10 after they read on their own. Guide practice, as needed. For teacher directions, see pages 122 and 123.

5. Homework 9: New Passage

The Pteranodon sailed over the stream, over the ferns and bushes.

Then he carried Jack down to the base of the oak tree.

When they came to a stop, Jack slid off the creature's back. And landed on the ground.

Then the Pteranodon took off again and glided into the sky.

"Bye, Henry," whispered Jack.

"Are you okay?" Annie shouted from the tree house.

Jack pushed his glasses into place. He kept staring up at the Pteranodon.

"Jack, are you okay?" Annie called.

Jack looked up at Annie. He smiled.

"Thanks for saving my life," he said. "That was really fun."

"Climb up!" said Annie.

Jack tried to stand. His legs were wobbly.

58

He felt a bit dizzy.

"Hurry!" shouted Annie. "He's coming!"

Jack looked around. The Tyrannosaurus was heading straight toward him!

Jack bolted to the ladder. He grabbed the sides and started up.

"Hurry! Hurry!" screamed Annie.

Jack scrambled into the tree house.

"He's coming toward the tree!" Annie cried.

Suddenly something slammed against the oak tree. The tree house shook like a leaf.

Jack and Annie tumbled into the books.

"Make a wish!" cried Annie.

"We need the book! The one with the picture of Frog Creek!" said Jack. "Where is it?"

He pushed some books aside. He had to find that book about Pennsylvania.

There it was!

59

He grabbed it and tore through it, looking for the photograph of the Frog Creek woods.

He found it! Jack pointed to the picture.

"I wish we could go home!" he shouted.

The wind began to moan. Softly at first.

"Hurry!" Jack yelled.

The wind picked up. It was whistling now.

The tree house started to spin.

It spun faster and faster.

Jack closed his eyes. He held on tightly to Annie.

Then everything was still.

Absolutely still.

60

ENTRY 9

COMPREHENSION PROCESSES
Understand, Apply, Create

WRITING TRAITS
Ideas and Content
Word Choice
Conventions—Complete Sentence,
Capital, Period
Presentation

Visualizing; Generating Ideas
Describing; Sentence Completion
Using Vocabulary—amazing, miracle

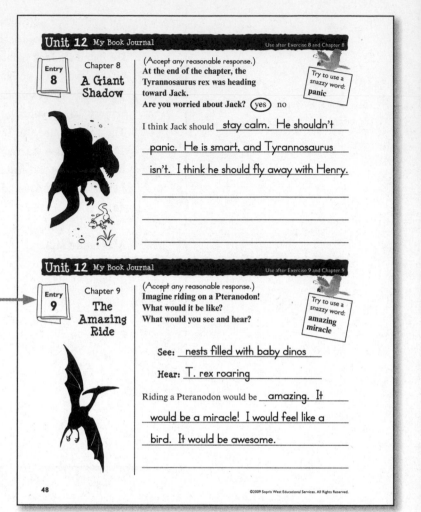

Unit 12 My Book Journal   Use after Exercise 8 and Chapter 8

Entry 8   Chapter 8   A Giant Shadow

(Accept any reasonable response.)
At the end of the chapter, the Tyrannosaurus rex was heading toward Jack.
Are you worried about Jack? (yes) no

Try to use a snazzy word: panic

I think Jack should stay calm. He shouldn't panic. He is smart, and Tyrannosaurus isn't. I think he should fly away with Henry.

Unit 12 My Book Journal   Use after Exercise 9 and Chapter 9

Entry 9   Chapter 9   The Amazing Ride

(Accept any reasonable response.)
Imagine riding on a Pteranodon!
What would it be like?
What would you see and hear?

Try to use a snazzy word: amazing miracle

See: nests filled with baby dinos

Hear: T. rex roaring

Riding a Pteranodon would be amazing. It would be a miracle! I would feel like a bird. It would be awesome.

48   ©2009 Sopris West Educational Services. All Rights Reserved.

PROCEDURES
For each step, demonstrate and guide practice, as needed. Then have students complete the page independently.

Creative Writing: Paragraph Writing—Specific Instructions

- Have students read the directions and then visualize what it would be like to ride on a Pteranodon.
  Read the sentences for Entry 9. (Imagine riding on a Pteranodon! What would it be like? What would you see and hear?)
  Everyone close your eyes and imagine that you are riding a Pteranodon. You are high in the air, miles above the ground. What are some things that you see? What are some things that you hear?

- Have students write words that describe what they would see and hear.
  Now, open your eyes. Let's talk about what you saw and heard. What are some things you saw while riding that Pteranodon? (I saw tops of trees, other dinosaurs on the ground, a large lake with dinosaurs in it, a colony of dinosaurs protecting their nests . . .)
  What did you hear? (birds, the wind swooshing, T. rex roaring)
  You can write any of the things you imagined next to "See" and "Hear."

- Have students write a short paragraph using what they imagined they saw and heard to describe what they imagined riding on a Pteranodon would be like. Encourage students to use the snazzy words "amazing" and "miracle" in their writing. Remind them to start sentences with a capital and end with a period or exclamation point.

Self-monitoring
Have students check and correct their work.

VISUALIZING AND ILLUSTRATING

COMPREHENSION PROCESSES

Remember, Understand

WRITING TRAITS

Conventions—Period

Identifying—What, Where
Visualizing, Illustrating

Comprehension Monitoring, Test Taking

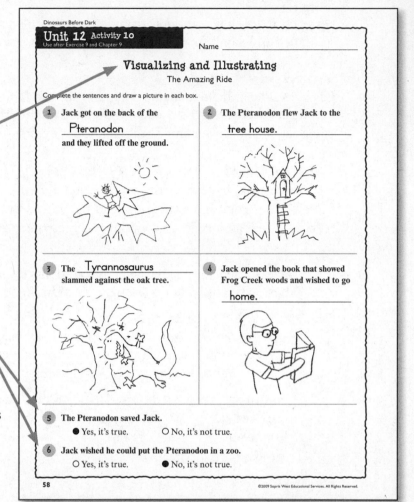

PROCEDURES

For each step, demonstrate and guide practice, as needed. Then have students complete the page independently.

1. Sentence Completion, Illustrating—Specific Instructions (Items 1–4)

- Have students read, complete, and illustrate each sentence.
- Encourage students to visualize what they will draw in each box and to include as many details as possible. Say something like:

  To illustrate the sentences in each box, you can first imagine, or visualize, what the sentences describe. Remember, visualizing helps you understand what you are reading.

  Read the first sentence to yourself, and figure out what goes in the blank.

  Everyone, read the sentence and orally fill in the blank.
  (Jack got on the back of the . . . *Pteranodon*, and they lifted off the ground.)
  Imagine what the Pteranodon looks like.
  What does it look like? (It has bat-like wings. It has a crest. It looks like an airplane . . .)
  Imagine Jack. What does he look like? (He has glasses. He is wearing long pants. He is carrying a notebook.)
  Those details will make your illustrations just great!
  When you start drawing, you can look in your book for more ideas.

- Remind students to end sentences with a period.

2. True/False: Selection Response (Items 5, 6)

❶ SOUND REVIEW
Use selected Sound Cards from Units 1–12.

❷ SHIFTY WORD BLENDING
For each word, have students say the underlined sound. Then have them sound out the word smoothly and say it. Use the words in sentences, as appropriate.

❸ SOUND PRACTICE
- For each task, have students spell and say the focus sound in the gray bar.
  Next, have students read each underlined sound, the word, then the whole column.
- Repeat with each column, building accuracy first, then fluency.

❹ ACCURACY AND FLUENCY BUILDING
- For each task, have students say any underlined part, then read the word.
- Set a pace. Then have students read the whole words in each task and column.
- Provide repeated practice, building accuracy first, then fluency.

B1. Contractions

Have students read "he will." Tell students the next word is a short way to say "he will." Then have students read the contraction. Repeat with "she'll" and "they'd."

D1. Multisyllabic Words
- For the list of words divided by syllables, have students read each syllable, then the whole word. Use the word in a sentence, as appropriate.
- For the list of whole words, build accuracy and then fluency.

simply	He didn't go into details. He said it quite . . . *simply.*
pocket	Gina had money in her . . . *pocket.*
distance	Locke couldn't see the house because it was too far in the . . . *distance.*
golden	The car was shiny and yellow. It almost looked . . . *golden.*

E1. Tricky Words
- For each Tricky Word, have students use the sounds and word parts they know to silently sound out the word. Use the word in a sentence to help with pronunciation.
- If the word is unfamiliar, tell students the word.

view	I couldn't see. The wall blocked my . . . *view.*
world	One day, I hope to travel around the . . . *world.*
course	Miss Tam was happy to do it. She said, "Of . . . *course* . . . I'll do it."
shoulder	The pirate had a parrot sitting on his . . . *shoulder.*
only	I have two sisters and . . . *only* . . . one brother.
tomorrow	We are not going to the zoo today. We are going . . . *tomorrow.*

- Have students go back and read the whole words in the column.

❺ MORPHOGRAPHS AND AFFIXES
- Have students read the underlined part, then the word.
- Repeat practice with whole words, mixing group and individual turns.
  Build accuracy, then fluency.

❻ GENERALIZATION: READING NEW WORDS IN PARAGRAPHS

- Have students read the paragraph silently, then out loud. Tell students to use the sounds and word parts they know to read any difficult words.
- Repeat practice, as needed.

Dinosaurs Before Dark

Unit 12 Exercise 10
Use before Chapter 10

1. SOUND REVIEW Use selected Sound Cards from Units 1–12.

2. SHIFTY WORD BLENDING For each word, have students say the underlined part, sound out smoothly, then read the word.

| d<u>aw</u>n | d<u>ew</u> | <u>k</u>new | kn<u>ow</u> | know<u>n</u> |

3. SOUND PRACTICE In each column, have students spell and say the sound, then say any underlined sound and the word. Next, have students read the whole column.

oi	ea, ee	igh	Bossy E
v<u>oi</u>ce	dr<u>ea</u>m	l<u>igh</u>t	d<u>a</u>zed
p<u>oi</u>nting	str<u>ee</u>t	br<u>igh</u>t	p<u>o</u>ked
j<u>oi</u>ned	p<u>ee</u>ked	s<u>igh</u>ed	st<u>a</u>red

4. ACCURACY AND FLUENCY BUILDING For each column, have students say any underlined part, then read each word. Next, have students read the whole column.

A1 Mixed Practice	B1 Contractions	C1 Word Endings	D1 Multisyllabic Words	E1 Tricky Words
r<u>oa</u>d	he will	<u>followed</u>	sim•ply	view
sl<u>u</u>ng	he'll	<u>whispered</u>	pock•et	world
t<u>i</u>ny		<u>clasped</u>	dis•tance	course
sin<u>ce</u>	she will		gold•en	shoulder
ting<u>le</u>	she'll	shrug		only
A2 Reading by Analogy	they would	shrugged	simply	tomorrow
onion	they'd		pocket	
million		engrave	distance	
medallion		engraving	golden	

5. MORPHOGRAPHS AND AFFIXES Have students read the underlined word part, then the word.

| Ⓐ | <u>ex</u>plain | <u>re</u>built | soft<u>ly</u> | <u>be</u>gan |
| Ⓑ | <u>before</u> | <u>ex</u>act | us<u>able</u> | <u>un</u>happy |

6. GENERALIZATION Have students read the paragraph silently, then out loud. (New words: distant, magic)

I looked out the window and saw a huge purple rabbit in a distant field. It hopped in front of some bushes. Then all of a sudden, it disappeared. I think it was a magic rabbit. I wished I had taken a picture. No one would ever believe my story.

47

CHAPTER 10 INSTRUCTIONS

Students read pages 61–64 with the teacher and pages 65–68 on their own.

COMPREHENSION PROCESSES

Remember, Understand, Apply

PROCEDURES

1. Reviewing Chapter 9

Explaining; Identifying—What

Discuss the questions from Chapter 9, Setting a Purpose.

Say something like:

Chapter 9 was exciting and full of suspense. Let's review what you found out.

What happened to the Pteranodon? (It dropped Jack off and flew away.)

What happened to the Tyrannosaurus? (He followed Jack to the tree.)

What happened to Jack and Annie? (They were in the tree house, but the Tyrannosaurus was slamming against the tree. They are still in danger.)

At the end of the chapter, what did Jack and Annie wish for? (They wished they could go home.)

2. Introducing Chapter 10

Identifying—Title; Predicting

This is the very last chapter. I'm going to be sorry the book has to end. I really enjoyed reading it. What's the title of this last chapter. (Home Before Dark)

What do you think is going to happen? (The kids will make it home.)

I think the kids will go home too. They need to be safe so they can be in other Tree House books!

3. First Reading

- Ask questions and discuss the story as indicated by the blue text in this teacher's guide.
- Mix group and individual turns, independent of your voice.
  Have students work toward a group accuracy goal of 0–3 errors.
  Quietly keep track of errors made by all students in the group.
- After reading the story, practice any difficult words.
  Reread the story if students have not reached the accuracy goal.

4. Second Reading, Timed Readings: Repeated Reading

- As time allows, have students do Timed Readings while others follow along.
- Time individuals for 30 seconds and encourage each child to work for a personal best.
- Determine words correct per minute. Record student scores.

10
Home Before Dark

A bird began to sing.

Jack opened his eyes. He was still pointing at the picture of the Frog Creek woods.

He peeked out the tree house window. Outside he saw the exact same view.

"We're home," whispered Annie.

The woods were lit with a golden late-afternoon light. The sun was about to set.

No time had passed since they'd left.

"Ja-ack! An-nie!" a voice called from the distance.

"That's Mom," said Annie, pointing.

61

Jack saw their mother far away. She was standing in front of their house. She looked very tiny.

"An-nie! Ja-ack!" she called.

62

After Reading Page 61

❶ **Understand:** Explaining—Where
Where are Jack and Annie?
(They are back in the Frog Creek woods.)

❷ **Understand:** Explaining
How do you know?
(Annie said, "We're home." They could hear their mother . . .)

❸ **Apply:** Inferring, Explaining
It says, "No time had passed since they'd left." A lot happened to Annie and Jack. How is it possible that it's still the same time as when they left?
(The tree house is magic. It's a make-believe story.)

Annie stuck her head out the window and shouted, "Come-ing!"

Jack still felt dazed. He just stared at Annie.

63

"What happened to us?" he said.

"We took a trip in a magic tree house," said Annie simply.

"But it's the same time as when we left," said Jack.

Annie shrugged.

"And how did it take us so far away?" said Jack. "And so long ago?"

"You just looked at a book and said you wished we could go there," said Annie. "And the magic tree house took us there."

"But *how?*" said Jack. "And who built this magic tree house? Who put all these books here?"

"A magic person, I guess," said Annie.

A magic person?

"Oh, look," said Jack. "I almost forgot about this." He reached into his pocket and pulled out the gold medallion. "Someone lost

64

After Reading Page 64
(Have students finish the sentence on page 65.)

❶ **Remember:** Identifying—What; Using Vocabulary—medallion
What did Jack find in his pocket?
(He found the gold medallion.)

128

CHAPTER 10 INSTRUCTIONS

Students read pages 65–68 without the teacher, independently or with partners.

COMPREHENSION PROCESSES

Understand, Apply, Evaluate

PREP NOTE

Setting a Purpose

Write questions on a chalkboard, white board, or large piece of paper before working with your small group.

PROCEDURES

1. Getting Ready

Have students turn to page 65.

2. Setting a Purpose

Explaining, Inferring, Responding

Before beginning reading, say something like:

As you read the last part of the book, ask yourselves the following questions:
- What is important about the medallion?
- What makes us think there will be other adventures?
- Ask yourself whether you would like to read other books by Mary Pope Osborne.

3. Reading on Your Own: Partner or Whisper Reading

- Have students take turns reading every other page with a partner, or have students whisper read pages 65–68 on their own.
- Continue having students track each word with their fingers.

4. Comprehension and Skill Work

Tell students that they will work on their Book Journal and do a Written Assessment after they read on their own. Guide practice, as needed. For teacher directions, see pages 132 and 133.

5. Homework 10: New Passage

this back there . . . in dinosaur land. Look, there's a letter M on it."

Annie's eyes got round. "You think *M* stands for *magic person?*" she said.

"I don't know," said Jack. "I just know someone went to that place before us."

"Ja-ack! An-nie!" came the distant cry again.

Annie poked her head out the window. "Come-ing!" she shouted.

Jack put the gold medallion back in his pocket.

He pulled the dinosaur book out of his pack. And put it back with all the other books.

Then he and Annie took one last look around the tree house.

"Good-bye, house," whispered Annie.

Jack slung his backpack over his shoulder. He pointed at the ladder.

65

Annie started down. Jack followed.

Seconds later they hopped onto the ground and started walking out of the woods.

"No one's going to believe our story," said Jack.

"So let's not tell anyone," said Annie.

"Dad won't believe it," said Jack.

"He'll say it was a dream," said Annie.

"Mom won't believe it," said Jack.

"She'll say it was pretend,"

"My teacher won't believe it," said Jack.

"She'll say you're nuts," said Annie.

"We better not tell anyone," said Jack.

"I already said that," said Annie.

Jack sighed. "I think I'm starting to not believe it myself," he said.

They left the woods and started up the road toward their house.

As they walked past all the houses on their street, the trip to dinosaur time *did* seem more and more like a dream.

Only *this* world and *this* time seemed real.

Jack reached into his pocket. He clasped the gold medallion.

67

He felt the engraving of the letter M. It made Jack's fingers tingle.

Jack laughed. Suddenly he felt very happy.

He couldn't explain what had happened today. But he knew for sure that their trip in the magic tree house had been real.

Absolutely real.

"Tomorrow," Jack said softly, "we'll go back to the woods."

"Of course," said Annie.

"And we'll climb up to the tree house," said Jack.

"Of course," said Annie.

"And we'll see what happens next," said Jack.

"Of course," said Annie. "Race you!"

And they took off together, running for home.

68

WRITTEN ASSESSMENT

COMPREHENSION PROCESSES

Remember, Understand, Apply

WRITING TRAITS

Word Choice
Conventions—Complete Sentence, Capital, Period
Presentation

Test Taking

Identifying—Main Character Sentence Completion

Identifying—Beginning

Identifying—Initiating Event

Inferring; Using Vocabulary—suspense

Identifying—Middle, Action

Unit 12 Written Assessment
(continued)

MAIN CHARACTER (1 point)
1 Who is the story about?

This story is about ___a Hadrosaurus mother.___

BEGINNING (1 point)
2 What happened at the beginning of the story?
- ● The Hadrosaurus munched on plants far away from her nest.
- ○ The Hadrosaurus munched on seeds near her babies.
- ○ The Hadrosaurus had wandered far from her nest to a new home.

INITIATING EVENT (1 point)
3 What startled the Hadrosaurus?
- ○ She looked around and saw her babies.
- ○ She saw dinosaurs running into the forest.
- ● She heard a loud booming noise and another Hadrosaurus bellowing.

INFERENCE, VOCABULARY–SUSPENSE (1 point)
4 In the middle of the story, there was a lot of excitement. We wondered what would happen next. The author created *suspense* by . . .
- ○ making us wonder whether the T. rex was dangerous.
- ● making us wonder whether the mother could save her babies.
- ○ making us wonder why the mother had left her babies.

MIDDLE–ACTION (1 point)
5 When the T. rex appeared, what did the mother Hadrosaurus do?
- ● She ran back to her nest to protect her babies.
- ○ She ran under the trees with the other dinosaurs.
- ○ She ran into the forest.

Turn the page.

©2009 Sopris West Educational Services. All Rights Reserved.

77

PROCEDURES

Do not demonstrate or guide practice.

Written Assessment—Introductory Instructions

1. Introduce the Written Assessment.
   - Remind students that their work today is an opportunity for them to show what they can do independently. Clarify your expectations, as needed.
   - Tell students they will whisper read the passage and then answer the questions without help.

Unit 12 Written Assessment

WARM-UP

Hadrosaurus

contentedly   swung   luscious   booming

The Hadrosaurus and the T. Rex

A mother Hadrosaurus munched contentedly on some luscious green plants. She had wandered far from her nest, but she knew her babies would be safe. After all, she was going to be gone for just a little while.

Suddenly, she heard a loud booming noise. Another Hadrosaurus bellowed. Startled, she lifted her head. She stood up high on her back legs. The dinosaurs were in a panic. Where was the danger? She sniffed the air and looked around with her sharp eyes.

A Tyrannosaurus rex burst out of the forest. The mother dinosaur knew she had to get back to her nest. She was frantic. She had to protect her babies! She started to run back to her nest.

The T. rex swung his head. He tried to grab a meal with his huge teeth. The dinosaurs ran. They were faster than the T. rex. The T. rex stopped running and wandered back to the forest. The mother and babies were safe.

76

continued

WRITTEN ASSESSMENT (*continued*)

Unit 12 Written Assessment (continued)

Inferring →

END–DRAWING CONCLUSIONS (1 point)

6 **In the end, the T. rex did not get a meal, and the babies were safe. What helped save the dinosaurs?**

○ The T. rex decided he was not hungry.
○ The T. rex could not see very well.
● The Hadrosaurus could run faster than the T. rex.

Inferring, Explaining, Sentence Writing →

INFERENCE–FACT (1 point) (Accept any reasonable response.)

7 **This story has a lot of information about dinosaurs. List one thing you learned about the Hadrosaurus.**

- herbivore—eats plants

Responding, Sentence Completion →

PERSONAL RESPONSE (1 point) (Accept any reasonable response.)

8 **What did you think about this story?**

I liked (liked / didn't like) this story because I learned how Hadrosaurus can run fast and protect itself. I'm glad the dinos were safe!

✓ Check and Correct

Reread your answers.
Do your answers make sense? ☑
Do you have a capital at the beginning of each sentence and a period at the end? ☑
Did you use your best handwriting? ☑

SCORING Date ______

Main Character 1 /1	Beginning 1 /1	Initiating Event 1 /1	Inference 1 /1
Middle Action 1 /1	End/Drawing Conclusions 1 /1	Inferring/Fact 1 /1	Personal Response 1 /1
			Total 8 /8

Teachers: If you wish to keep a cumulative record of student assessment scores, see the *Assessment Manual.*

78 ©2009 Sopris West Educational Services. All Rights Reserved.

2. Check for student understanding.
   Say something like:
   Look at your assessment. What are you going to do first? (write my name)

   What are going to do next? (whisper read the passage)
   What will you do after you read the passage? (answer the questions)

   That's great. Now what will you do if you get to a hard question?
   (reread the question and try again)
   That's right. What should you do if it's still hard? (reread the passage and try again)
   Very good. And if you still aren't sure, what will you do? (do my best and keep going)

3. Remind students to check and correct.
   When you finish your assessment, what should you do? (check and correct)
   That's right. Go to the top of the page. Reread the questions and make sure your answers make sense. Fix anything that doesn't sound right. Make sure you have an answer for every question.

4. Remind students what to do when they finish their work.

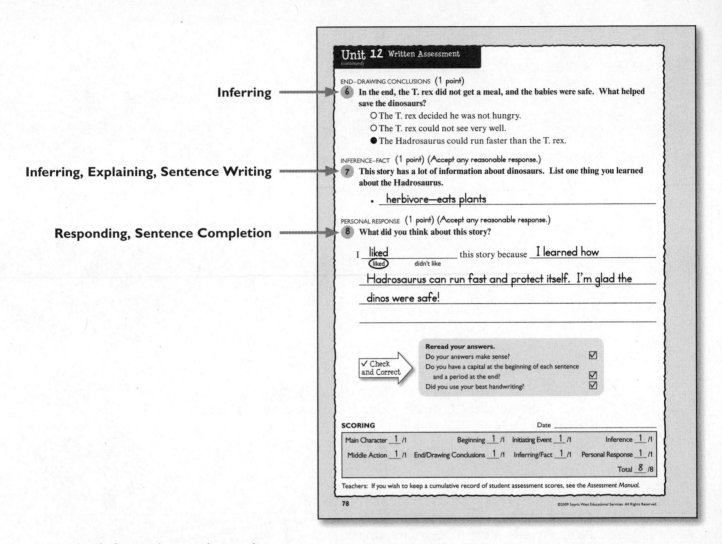

End of the Unit

In this section, you will find:

Making Decisions

As you near the end of the unit, plan to give the Written Assessment and the Oral Reading Fluency Assessment to each child in your group. Use this section as a general guide for making instructional decisions and doing diagnostic planning.

Written Assessment

The Unit 12 Written Assessment is located on page 76 of *Activity Book 2* and on the CD.

Oral Reading Fluency Assessment

The Unit 12 Oral Reading Fluency Assessment is located on page 139 of this teacher's guide and in the *Assessment Manual*. Note that there is also an optional mid-unit Oral Reading Fluency Assessment on page 138.

Certificate of Achievement

Celebrate your children's accomplishments. When your students master the unit skills, send home the Certificate of Achievement.

Goal Setting • Fluency

Through goal setting, help your students recognize their accomplishments and learn how to be self-directed learners.

Extra Practice Lessons

Use the Extra Practice lessons for students who need additional decoding and fluency work. Student materials can be copied from the Extra Practice blackline masters.

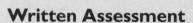

Making Decisions

GENERAL ASSESSMENT GUIDELINES

> **OPTIONAL MID-UNIT ASSESSMENT**
>
> For students who require careful monitoring (lowest-performing students in the group), give the mid-unit Oral Reading Fluency Assessment found on page 138.

1. After students read Story Reading 10, Chapter 10 of *Dinosaurs Before Dark*, give the group the Unit 12 Written Assessment in place of Comprehension and Skill Work. Follow the instructions on pages 132 and 133 of this guide.

2. While the group is completing the Written Assessment or any time during the day, administer the Oral Reading Fluency Assessment. Assess each student individually.

   Optional: Graph the results of the assessment. (See Unit 7 Teacher's Guide, pages 92 and 95.)
   • If the student's words correct per minute go up, congratulate the student.
   • If the student's words correct per minute go down, discuss the student's overall improvement and help him or her identify ways to improve for the next assessment.

3. Score oral fluency responses on the Student Assessment Record. Adhere to the scoring criteria in the *Assessment Manual*. Use a stopwatch to time how long it takes each student to read the Oral Reading Fluency Passage, and record errors.

USING WRITTEN ASSESSMENT RESULTS

Results of the Written Assessment *should not* be used to determine whether a student or group of students continues forward in the program. As long as students pass the Oral Reading Fluency Assessment, they should continue forward with the next unit.

The Written Assessment should be used to informally monitor how well students read independently and answer questions in writing. If any student has difficulty with the Written Assessment, re-administer the assessment orally.

If the student has difficulty answering the questions orally:
• Record the types of errors (e.g., main idea, sequencing, open-ended response).
• Provide explicit instruction for these types of questions during reading group, before independent work, and in tutorials, as needed.
   1) Demonstrate (or model) appropriate responses, guide practice, and provide opportunities for independent practice.
   2) For inferential questions, think aloud with students—explain how you arrive at an answer.
   3) For literal questions, teach students to reread a passage, locate information, reread the question, and respond.

USING THE ORAL READING FLUENCY RESULTS

At the end of each unit, you will need to make decisions regarding student progress. Should students go forward in the program? Does the group need Extra Practice before proceeding? Do individuals require more assistance and practice to continue working in their group? These decisions all require use of the oral reading fluency data and professional judgment. As you analyze assessment results, watch for trends and anomalies.

See the *Assessment Manual* for detailed information and instructional recommendations. General guidelines and recommendations follow:

Strong Pass ≥ 112 WCPM 0–2 errors	• Continue with the current pace of instruction. • Have students set goals. (Until students are reading approximately 180 words correct per minute, oral reading fluency continues to be an instructional goal.)
Pass 91–111 WCPM 0–2 errors	• Continue with the current pace of instruction. Consider increasing fluency practice.
No Pass ≤ 90 WCPM	• If a child scores a No Pass but has previously passed all assessments, you may wish to advance the student to the next unit, then carefully monitor the student. • If a child scores a No Pass but has previously passed all assessments, you may wish to advance the student to the next unit and also provide additional practice opportunities. (See below.) • If a child scores two consecutive No Passes or periodic No Passes, additional practice must be provided. (See below.) • If a child scores three consecutive No Passes, the student should be placed in a lower-performing group.

RED FLAG
A No Pass is a red flag. A mild early intervention can prevent an intense and time-consuming intervention in the future.

Added Practice Options for Groups
Warm-Ups:
• Begin each lesson with Partner Reading of the previous day's homework.
• Begin each day with Partner Reading of a Word Fluency from Extra Practice.
• Begin each lesson with a five-minute Fluency Booster. Place copies of the Unit 7–11 *Read Well* Homework in three-ring notebooks. Each day, have students begin Finger Tracking and Whisper Reading at Unit 7, Homework 1. At the end of five minutes, have students mark where they are in their notebooks. The next day, the goal is to read farther.
• Begin each Story Reading with a review of the previous day's story.
• After reading the story, include Short Passage Practice on a daily basis.

Extended Units: If several children begin to score No Passes or barely pass, extend the unit by adding Extra Practices 1, 2, and/or 3. Extra Practice lessons include Decoding Practice, Fluency Passage, Word Fluency, and a Comprehension and Skill Activity. (See pages 142–153 in this guide.)

Jell-Well Reviews: A Jell-Well Review is the *Read Well* term for a review of earlier units. A Jell-Well Review is a period of time taken to celebrate what children have learned and an opportunity to firm up their foundation of learning. To complete a Jell-Well Review, take the group back to the last unit for which all students scored Strong Passes. Then quickly cycle back up. See the *Assessment Manual* for how to build a Jell-Well Review.

Added Practice Options for Individual Students

Tutorials: Set up five-minute tutorials on a daily basis with an assistant, trained volunteer, or cross-age tutor. Have the tutor provide Short Passage Practice and Timed Readings or Extra Practice lessons.

Double Dose: Find ways to provide a double dose of *Read Well* instruction.

• Have the student work in his or her group *and* a lower-performing group.

• Have an instructional assistant, older student, or parent volunteer preview or review lessons.

• Have an instructional assistant provide instruction with Extra Practice lessons.

• Preview new lessons or review previous lessons.

END-OF-THE-UNIT CELEBRATION

When students pass the Oral Reading Fluency Assessment, celebrate with the Certificate of Achievement on page 140.

Note: Using the Flesch-Kincaid Grade Level readability formula, both the Unit 12 optional mid-unit Assessment and the end-of-unit Assessment have a 2.6 readability level. Readabilities are based on number of words per sentence and number of syllables per word. Adding one or two multisyllabic words can increase readability by a month or two. Though we are attending to readability for the assessments, the overriding factor is decodability.

GOAL SETTING

If you choose to have students set goals:

• Copy a goal-setting form from page 141 for each student and write in students' names.

• For each student, fill in the blanks. The goal for the next unit should be 2 words per minute more than the fluency score in this unit.

• Guide students through the form. Say something like:
Read the sentences at the top. (I am a master reader. I read the book Dinosaurs Before Dark and wrote my own book journal about the story. I can read any story, big or small!)

You are master readers. It's awesome that you read *Dinosaurs Before Dark*!

Your goal-setting forms say, "Since the beginning of the year, I've improved my reading by *blank* words per minute." Everyone, look at your form. It tells you how many words you've improved by since the beginning of the year. [Jan], how many words have you improved by? (30)

Wow! That is very, very impressive.

[Jasmine], what does *impressive* mean? (It means that I should be proud of myself.)

Yes, that's exactly right. You've all made great gains, and you should be proud of yourselves.

• Help students be in control of their progress by helping them identify what actions they can take to meet their goal.

TRICKY WORD and FOCUS SKILL WARM-UP

imagine	ancient	choice	reptile	laughed	above

ORAL READING FLUENCY PASSAGE

A Pretend Pteranodon

★Cole read lots of books. He loved to study ancient   10
reptiles and dinosaurs. He liked to imagine what it would be like   22
to meet one.   25

"If you could meet an ancient creature, which one would   35
you choose?" Cole asked everyone he saw.   42

Cole knew what his choice would be. He really wanted to   53
meet a Pteranodon. He could almost see one soaring high above   64
the treetops. He could imagine hearing its loud, screeching call.   74

"Look at those giant wings," Cole said as he pointed to the   86
large picture in his book. "I want to ride on a Pteranodon."   98

"Let's pretend, Cole," said Lilly. Cole's sister loved to   107
pretend. She scrambled onto the bed, spread her arms wide, and   118
jumped.   119

"Look, Cole. I'm flying!" shouted Lilly as she flapped her   129
arms.   130

Cole laughed. Then he sighed and turned back to his   140
dinosaur book.   142

ORAL READING FLUENCY	Start timing at the ★. Mark errors. Make a single slash in the text (/) at 60 seconds. If the student completes the passage in less than 60 seconds, have the student go back to the ★ and continue reading. Make a double slash (//) in the text at 60 seconds.
WCPM	Determine words correct per minute by subtracting errors from words read in 60 seconds.
STRONG PASS	The student scores no more than 2 errors on the first pass through the passage and reads 112 or more words correct per minute. Continue with Unit 12.
PASS	The student scores no more than 2 errors on the first pass through the passage and reads 91 to 111 words correct per minute. Continue with Unit 12.
NO PASS	The student scores 3 or more errors on the first pass through the passage and/or reads 90 or fewer words correct per minute. Provide added fluency practice with Chapters 1–5, *Dinosaurs Before Dark*.

TRICKY WORD and FOCUS SKILL WARM-UP

imagine	heard	straight	toward	reptile	valley

ORAL READING FLUENCY PASSAGE

Franny and Paul

★What would Pteranodons say if they could talk? Let's   9
imagine.   10

"How are your babies, Franny?" asked Paul. The two   19
reptiles were soaring through the air. They glanced down at the   30
nests in the valley.   34

"My babies are growing. I am bringing them plants to   44
eat," said Franny proudly. Franny shouted to her babies, "I'm   54
coming! Food's on the way!"   59

Franny pointed her head toward the nest. Paul said, "Soon   69
they will be ready to get their own food."   78

Paul spread his giant wings again. He started to fly   88
away when he saw a horrible sight. A stampede! Hundreds of   99
dinosaurs were scrambling through the valley. They were in   108
a panic. Paul heard a loud roar. It was Rex, the meat-eating   121
dinosaur everyone feared.   124

"Hurry home!" said Paul to Franny. "Rex is hunting!"   133
Franny nodded and flew straight down to her nest.   142

ORAL READING FLUENCY	Start timing at the ★. Mark errors. Make a single slash in the text (/) at 60 seconds. Have the student complete the passage. If the student completes the passage in less than 60 seconds, have the student go back to the ★ and continue reading. Make a double slash (//) in the text at 60 seconds.
WCPM	Determine words correct per minute by subtracting errors from words read in 60 seconds.
STRONG PASS	The student scores no more than 2 errors on the first pass through the passage and reads 112 or more words correct per minute. Proceed to Unit 13.
PASS	The student scores no more than 2 errors on the first pass through the passage and reads 91 to 111 words correct per minute. Proceed to Unit 13.
NO PASS	The student scores 3 or more errors on the first pass through the passage and/or reads 90 or fewer words correct per minute. Provide added fluency practice with *RW2* Unit 12 Extra Practice. (Lessons follow the certificate at the end of the teacher's guide.) After completing the Extra Practice, retest the student.

Absolutely Awesome!

_____

has successfully completed

Read Well 2 Unit 12 • Dinosaurs Before Dark

with _____ words correct per minute.

Teacher Signature _____

Date _____

Absolutely Awesome!

_____

has successfully completed

Read Well 2 Unit 12 • Dinosaurs Before Dark

with _____ words correct per minute.

Teacher Signature _____

Date _____

Goal Setting · Fluency

I am a master reader. I read the book *Dinosaurs Before Dark* and wrote my own book journal about the story. I can read any story, big or small!

My goal for Unit 13 is _____ words correct per minute.

I can work to reach my goal by:

- Reading and rereading carefully

- Working hard in reading group

- _____
  _____

Signed _____

Date _____

My Personal Best:

In Unit 12, I read _____ words correct per minute.

Since the beginning of the year, I've improved my reading by _____ words per minute. That's wonderful!

Goal Setting · Fluency

I am a master reader. I read the book *Dinosaurs Before Dark* and wrote my own book journal about the story. I can read any story, big or small!

My goal for Unit 13 is _____ words correct per minute.

I can work to reach my goal by:

- Reading and rereading carefully

- Working hard in reading group

- _____
  _____

Signed _____

Date _____

My Personal Best:

In Unit 12, I read _____ words correct per minute.

Since the beginning of the year, I've improved my reading by _____ words per minute. That's wonderful!

PROCEDURES

1. **Sound Review**

   Use selected Sound Cards from Units 1–12.

2. **Sounding Out Smoothly**
   - For each word, have students say the underlined part, sound out the word smoothly, then read the whole word. (Use the words in sentences, as needed.)
   - Have students read all the words in the row, building accuracy first, then fluency.
   - Repeat practice. Mix group and individual turns, independent of your voice.

3. **Accuracy and Fluency Building**
   - For each task, have students say any underlined part, then read each word.
   - Set a pace. Then have students read the whole words in each task and column.
   - Provide repeated practice, building accuracy first, then fluency.

4. **Tricky Words**

   Have students read each row for accuracy, then fluency.

5. **Multisyllabic Words**

   For each word, have students read each syllable out loud, then tell how many syllables are in the word. If needed, use the word in a sentence. Have students read the whole word.

6. **Dictation**

   brown, frown, found, should, would, could
   - Say "brown." Have students say the word. Have students touch or write the sounds, then read the word. Say something like:

   The first word is **brown.** Say the word. (brown)

   What's the first sound? (/b/) Touch under /b/.
   What's the next sound? (/rrr/) Touch under /rrr/.
   What's the next sound? (/ow/) Write /ow/ with the <u>o-w</u> pattern.
   What's the last sound? (/nnn/) Touch under /nnn/.
   Read the word. (brown)

   - Repeat with "frown" and "found."
   - Continue with the rhyming words: should, would, could.

Unit 12 Decoding Practice

Name _____

1. SOUND REVIEW Use selected Sound Cards from *Read Well 2*, Units 1–12.

2. SOUNDING OUT SMOOTHLY Have students say the underlined part, sound out and read each word, then read the row.

o<u>dd</u>	<u>hea</u>d	<u>kn</u>elt	f<u>er</u>n

3. ACCURACY/FLUENCY BUILDING Have students say any underlined part, then read each word. Next, have students read the column.

A1 Sound Practice	**B1** Word Endings	**C1** Bossy <u>E</u>	**D1** Compound Words
h<u>au</u>l	repl<u>y</u>	cl<u>o</u>ser	everyone
l<u>au</u>nch	repli<u>ed</u>	t<u>i</u>le	something
l<u>au</u>ndry		rept<u>i</u>le	maybe
	<u>ask</u>ed		
<u>gi</u>ant	<u>dash</u>ed	b<u>o</u>ne	**D2** Multisyllabic Words
en<u>gi</u>ne	<u>vanish</u>ed	bony	creature
A2 Mixed Practice	<u>reach</u>ed		lizard
nev<u>er</u>	<u>glance</u>d	sh<u>a</u>ke	wonder
n<u>ear</u>by		shaking	
g<u>ol</u>den	<u>point</u>ed		
	<u>start</u>ed	sc<u>a</u>re	
		scaring	

4. TRICKY WORDS Have students read each row for accuracy, then read the entire grid for fluency.

touch	sure	heard	are	was	5
come	coming	walked	again	said	10

5. MULTISYLLABIC WORDS Have students read the word by parts, tell how many syllables are in the word, then read the whole word.

Ⓐ	stam•pede	stampede	i•ma•gine	imagine
Ⓑ	hor•ri•ble	horrible	un•der•stood	understood
Ⓒ	sud•den•ly	suddenly	cau•tious•ly	cautiously

6. DICTATION Say the word. Guide students as they say and segment the word. Have students say each sound as they touch or write it.

A1 Shifty Words	**B1** Rhyming Words
b r <u>o</u> <u>w</u> n	sh <u>o</u> <u>u</u> <u>l</u> d
f r <u>o</u> w n	w <u>o</u> <u>u</u> <u>l</u> d
f ou n <u>d</u>	c <u>o</u> <u>u</u> <u>l</u> d

82

143

PROCEDURES

1. First Reading

Mix group and individual turns, independent of your voice. Have students work toward an accuracy goal of 0–2 errors and practice any difficult words.

2. Second Reading, Short Passage Practice: Developing Prosody

- Demonstrate how to read a line or two with expression. Read at a rate slightly faster than the students' rate. Say something like:

  Listen as I read the first two sentences with expression and phrasing. I'm going to emphasize certain words and pause between sentences.

  "Playing by the stream, Franny and Paul heard something in the nearby ferns. 'What's that?' Franny asked."

- Guide practice with your voice. **Now read the paragraph with me.**

- Provide individual turns while others track with their fingers and whisper read. Provide descriptive and positive feedback.

  [Jerry], you read with wonderful expression!

EXTRA PRACTICE 1

Unit 12 Fluency Passage

Name _____

Fluency Passage

My goal is to read with 0–2 errors and ____ words correct per minute.

I read with ____ errors and ____ words correct per minute.

The Creature That Vanished

Playing by the stream, Franny and Paul heard something in the	11
nearby ferns.	13
"What's that?" Franny asked. Franny walked closer to the ferns and	24
found an odd-looking creature looking at her. It was golden brown with	37
a bony crest on its head. It looked like a strange lizard.	49
"What is it?" asked Paul.	54
"I am not sure," replied Franny. As Paul came closer to the creature,	67
it started shaking.	70
"I think you are scaring it," said Franny.	78
"I wonder if it's a reptile," Paul said. Franny knelt down and	90
cautiously reached out and touched its skin.	97
"Its skin is soft," she said. "Not hard like a reptile."	108
"Maybe we should catch it," said Paul.	115
Suddenly, as if it understood what they said, the creature dashed and	127
vanished. Paul and Franny never saw the creature again.	136

Homework
I've listened to my child read this passage twice. Date _____ Signed _____

©2009 Sopris West Educational Services. All Rights Reserved.   83

3. Partner Reading: Repeated Reading (Checkout Opportunity)

 While students do Partner Reading, listen to individuals read the passage. Work on accuracy and fluency, as needed.

4. Homework: Repeated Reading

 Have students read the story at home.

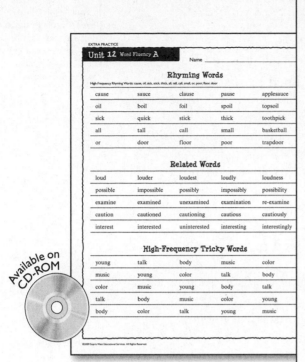

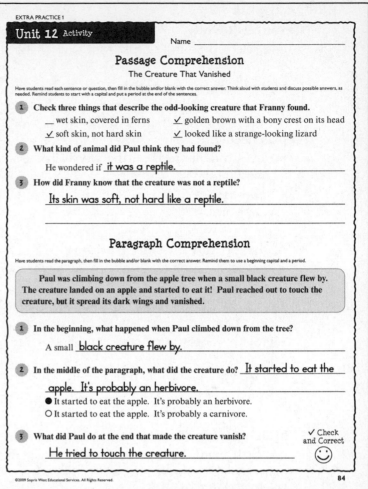

PROCEDURES

For each step, demonstrate and guide practice, as needed. Then have students complete the page independently.

1. Activity

Passage Comprehension

- Have students read each sentence or question, then fill in the bubble and/or blank, or check the blank with the correct answer.
- Think aloud with students and discuss the multiple-choice options, as needed.

Paragraph Comprehension

- Have students read the paragraph.
- Have students read each numbered sentence, then fill in the bubble and/or blank.
- Have students read the completed sentences.

Self-monitoring

Have students read and check their work, then draw a happy face in the Check and Correct circle.

2. Word Fluency (BLMs are located on the CD.)

- To build fluency, have students read Rhyming Words, Related Words, and High-Frequency Tricky Words. Have students read each section three times in a row.
- To build accuracy, have students read all sets with partners.

> **ACCURACY BEFORE FLUENCY (Reminder)**
>
> Word Fluency is designed to build accuracy and fluency. Students should practice for accuracy before working on fluency.

PROCEDURES

1. Sound Review

Use selected Sound Cards from Units 1–12.

2. Sounding Out Smoothly

- For each word, have students say the underlined part, sound out the word smoothly, then read the whole word. (Use the words in sentences, as needed.)
- Have students read all the words in the row, building accuracy first, then fluency.
- Repeat practice. Mix group and individual turns, independent of your voice.

3. Accuracy and Fluency Building

- For each task, have students say any underlined part, then read each word.
- Set a pace. Then have students read the whole words in each task and column.
- Provide repeated practice, building accuracy first, then fluency.

4. Tricky Words

Have students read each row for accuracy, then fluency.

5. Multisyllabic Words

For each word, have students read each syllable out loud, then tell how many syllables are in the word. If needed, use the word in a sentence. Have students read the whole word.

6. Dictation

roar, wore, more, meat, heat, seat

- Say "roar." Have students say the word. Have students touch or write the sounds, then read the word.

  The first word is **roar.** Say the word. (roar)

  What's the first sound? (/rrr/) Touch under /rrr/.
  What's the next sound? (/ōōō/) Write /ōōō/ with the o-a pattern.
  What's the last sound? (/rrr/) Touch under /rrr/.
  Read the word. (roar)

- Repeat with "wore" and "more."
- Continue with the rhyming words: meat, heat, seat.

The CAUTION box:

CAUTION
Your children may not need Extra Practice. Use assessment results to determine if Extra Practice is needed.

EXTRA PRACTICE 2

Unit 12 Decoding Practice

Name _____

1. SOUND REVIEW Use selected Sound Cards from *Read Well 2*, Units 1–12.

2. SOUNDING OUT SMOOTHLY Have students say the underlined part, sound out and read each word, then read the row.

f<u>lew</u>	sp<u>rea</u>d	<u>oa</u>k	p<u>oi</u>nt

3. ACCURACY/FLUENCY BUILDING Have students say any underlined part, then read each word. Next, have students read the column.

A1 Sound Practice	**B1** Word Endings	**C1** Rhyming Words	**D1** Compound Words
P<u>au</u>l	try	s<u>aw</u>	another
c<u>au</u>se	tried	dr<u>aw</u>	outside
f<u>au</u>lt	cry	str<u>aw</u>	himself
	cried		myself
litt<u>le</u>		**C2** Bossy E	
scramb<u>le</u>	st<u>ea</u>dy	n<u>o</u>se	**D2** Multisyllabic Words
stumb<u>led</u>	steadied	h<u>o</u>me	hundreds
grumb<u>led</u>		c<u>a</u>me	giant
horrib<u>le</u>	<u>dragg</u>ed	m<u>a</u>de	pretend
	<u>nodd</u>ed	l<u>i</u>ked	valley
	<u>curv</u>ed	rept<u>i</u>le	ready

4. TRICKY WORDS Have students read each row for accuracy, then read the entire grid for fluency.

toward	straight	course	caught	wanted	5
climbed	build	thought	through	brother	10

5. MULTISYLLABIC WORDS Have students read the word by parts, tell how many syllables are in the word, then read the whole word.

Ⓐ	di•no•saurs	dinosaurs	e•nor•mous	enormous
Ⓑ	dan•ger•ous	dangerous	rhi•no•cer•os	rhinoceros
Ⓒ	Tri•cer•a•tops	Triceratops	Pter•an•o•don	Pteranodon

6. DICTATION Say the word. Guide students as they say and segment the word. Have students say each sound as they touch or write it.

A1 Shifty Words	**B1** Rhyming Words
r <u>o a</u> r	m <u>ea</u> t
<u>w</u> o r e	h <u>ea</u> t
<u>m</u> o r e	s <u>ea</u> t

85

PROCEDURES

1. First Reading

Mix group and individual turns, independent of your voice. Have students work toward an accuracy goal of 0–2 errors and practice any difficult words.

2. Second Reading, Timed Reading: Repeated Reading

- Once the group accuracy goal has been achieved, time individual students for 30 or 60 seconds while the other children track with their fingers and whisper read.
- Determine words correct per minute. Record student scores. Celebrate when students reach their goals!

  Wow! [Sophie], you met your goal. That was your best score ever. You get to read to the principal this week.

3. Partner Reading: Repeated Reading (Checkout Opportunity)

While students do Partner Reading, listen to individuals read the passage. Work on accuracy and fluency, as needed.

4. Homework: Repeated Reading

Have students read the story at home.

EXTRA PRACTICE 2

Unit 12 Fluency Passage

Name _____

Fluency Passage

My goal is to read with 0–2 errors and ____ words correct per minute.

I read with ____ errors and ____ words correct per minute.

Pretend Pteranodon

My little brother, Paul, liked to pretend to be a dinosaur. One week,	13
he wore a big curved horn on his nose. "What are you, a rhinoceros?" I	28
asked.	29
"I'm a Triceratops, of course," he said.	36
Another time, Paul went too far and tried to be a Pteranodon. He	49
made a pair of giant, bat-like wings, then dragged them over to the	63
enormous oak tree. When he climbed up into the tree, the wings caught	76
on the first branch. Paul stumbled and then steadied himself. Just then,	88
Mom came outside and saw him in the tree.	97
"That's too dangerous!" she cried. "Get down right now! It would be	109
horrible if you fell!"	113
As Paul started down, he grumbled, "I was just going to build a	126
nest."	127
I thought to myself, "I think he wanted to spread his wings and fly!"	141

Homework

I've listened to my child read this passage twice.   Date _____   Signed _____

86

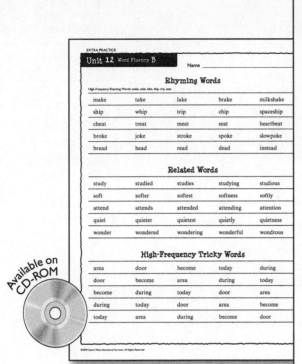

EXTRA PRACTICE
Unit 12 Word Fluency B

Name _____

Rhyming Words

High-Frequency Rhyming Words: make, take, bike, ship, chip, seat

make	take	lake	brake	milkshake
ship	whip	trip	chip	spaceship
cheat	treat	meat	seat	heartbeat
broke	joke	stroke	spoke	slowpoke
bread	head	read	dead	instead

Related Words

study	studied	studies	studying	studious
soft	softer	softest	softness	softly
attend	attends	attended	attending	attention
quiet	quieter	quietest	quietly	quietness
wonder	wondered	wondering	wonderful	wondrous

High-Frequency Tricky Words

area	door	become	today	during
door	become	area	during	today
become	during	today	door	area
during	today	door	area	become
today	area	during	become	door

©2009 Sopris West Educational Services. All Rights Reserved.

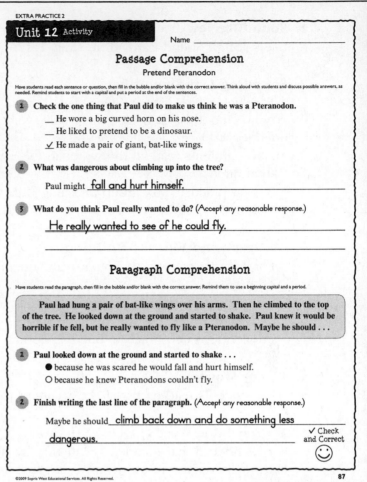

EXTRA PRACTICE 2

Unit 12 Activity

Name _____

Passage Comprehension
Pretend Pteranodon

Have students read each sentence or question, then fill in the bubble and/or blank with the correct answer. Think aloud with students and discuss possible answers, as needed. Remind students to start with a capital and put a period at the end of the sentences.

1 **Check the one thing that Paul did to make us think he was a Pteranodon.**
   __ He wore a big curved horn on his nose.
   __ He liked to pretend to be a dinosaur.
   ✓ He made a pair of giant, bat-like wings.

2 **What was dangerous about climbing up into the tree?**
   Paul might fall and hurt himself.

3 **What do you think Paul really wanted to do?** (Accept any reasonable response.)
   He really wanted to see of he could fly.

Paragraph Comprehension

Have students read the paragraph, then fill in the bubble and/or blank with the correct answer. Remind them to use a beginning capital and a period.

> Paul had hung a pair of bat-like wings over his arms. Then he climbed to the top of the tree. He looked down at the ground and started to shake. Paul knew it would be horrible if he fell, but he really wanted to fly like a Pteranodon. Maybe he should . . .

1 **Paul looked down at the ground and started to shake . . .**
   ● because he was scared he would fall and hurt himself.
   ○ because he knew Pteranodons couldn't fly.

2 **Finish writing the last line of the paragraph.** (Accept any reasonable response.)
   Maybe he should climb back down and do something less dangerous.

   ✓ Check and Correct
   ☺

©2009 Sopris West Educational Services. All Rights Reserved.   87

PROCEDURES

For each step, demonstrate and guide practice, as needed. Then have students complete the page independently.

1. Activity
Passage Comprehension
- Have students read each sentence or question, then fill in or check the blank with the correct answer.
- Think aloud with students and discuss the multiple-choice options, as needed.

Paragraph Comprehension
- Have students read the paragraph.
- Have students read each numbered sentence, then fill in the bubble and blank.
- Have students read the completed sentences.

Self-monitoring
Have students read and check their work, then draw a happy face in the Check and Correct circle.

2. Word Fluency (BLMs are located on the CD.)
- To build fluency, have students read Rhyming Words, Related Words, and High-Frequency Tricky Words. Have students read each section three times in a row.
- To build accuracy, have students read all sets with partners.

> **ACCURACY BEFORE FLUENCY (Reminder)**
>
> Word Fluency is designed to build accuracy and fluency. Students should practice for accuracy before working on fluency.

PROCEDURES

1. **Sound Review**

   Use selected Sound Cards from Units 1–12.

2. **Sounding Out Smoothly**
   - For each word, have students say the underlined part, sound out the word smoothly, then read the whole word. (Use the words in sentences, as needed.)
   - Have students read all the words in the row, building accuracy first, then fluency.
   - Repeat practice. Mix group and individual turns, independent of your voice.

3. **Accuracy and Fluency Building**
   - For each task, have students say any underlined part, then read each word.
   - Set a pace. Then have students read the whole words in each task and column.
   - Provide repeated practice, building accuracy first, then fluency.

4. **Tricky Words**

   Have students read each row for accuracy, then fluency.

5. **Multisyllabic Words**

   For each word, have students read each syllable out loud, then tell how many syllables are in the word. If needed, use the word in a sentence. Have students read the whole word.

6. **Dictation**

   proud, loud, load, pick, thick, quick
   - Say "proud." Have students say the word. Have students touch or write the sounds, then read the word. Say something like:
   The first word is **proud.** Say the word. (proud)

   What's the first sound? (/p/) Touch under /p/.
   What's the next sound? (/rrr/) Touch under /rrr/.
   What's the next sound? (/ou/) Write /ou/ with the <u>o-u</u> pattern.
   What's the last sound? (/d/) Touch under /d/.

   Read the word. (proud)

   - Repeat with "loud" and "load."
   - Continue with the rhyming words: pick, thick, quick.

EXTRA PRACTICE 3

Unit 12 Decoding Practice

Name _____

1. SOUND REVIEW Use selected Sound Cards from *Read Well 2*, Units 1–12.

2. SOUNDING OUT SMOOTHLY Have students say the underlined part, sound out and read each word, then read the row.

s<u>igh</u>t	<u>Pau</u>l	<u>air</u>	gla<u>nce</u>

3. ACCURACY/FLUENCY BUILDING Have students say any underlined part, then read each word. Next, have students read the column.

A1 Mixed Practice	**B1** Word Endings	**C1** Rhyming Words	**D1** Related Words
gl<u>ea</u>med	shine	sh<u>ine</u>	engr<u>a</u>ve
f<u>ea</u>red	shiny	l<u>ine</u>	engraved
pr<u>ou</u>dly		f<u>ine</u>	engraving
sh<u>ou</u>ted	baby	m<u>ine</u>	**D2** Multisyllabic Words
s<u>oar</u>ing	babies	**C2** Compound Words	belongs
gr<u>ow</u>ing	hurry	something	trophy
bri<u>ng</u>ing	hurried	sunlight	panic
hol<u>d</u>ing		backpack	away
ima<u>g</u>ine	scramble	upset	picture
	scrambling		

4. TRICKY WORDS Have students read each row for accuracy, then read the entire grid for fluency.

words	lives	who	straight	eye	5
your	toward	two	caught	front	10

5. MULTISYLLABIC WORDS Have students read the word by parts, tell how many syllables are in the word, then read the whole word.

Ⓐ	li•brar•y	library	fam•i•ly	family
Ⓑ	re•mem•ber	remember	prob•a•bly	probably
Ⓒ	me•dal•lion	medallion	ex•am•ined	examined

6. DICTATION Say the word. Guide students as they say and segment the word. Have students say each sound as they touch or write it.

A1 Shifty Words	**B1** Rhyming Words
pr<u>ou</u>d l<u>ou</u>d l<u>oa</u>d	p<u>i</u>ck th<u>i</u>ck qu<u>i</u>ck

88

PROCEDURES

1. First Reading

Mix group and individual turns, independent of your voice. Have students work toward an accuracy goal of 0–2 errors and practice any difficult words.

2. Second Reading, Short Passage Practice: Developing Prosody

- Demonstrate how to read a line or two with expression. Read at a rate slightly faster than the students' rate. Say something like:

  Listen as I read the first two sentences with expression and phrasing. I'm going to emphasize certain words and pause between sentences.

  "When I was walking home from the library, something shiny in the grass caught my eye. I picked it up and examined it."

- Guide practice with your voice. Now read the paragraph with me.

- Provide individual turns while others track with their fingers and whisper read. Provide descriptive and positive feedback.

  [Anand], you read with wonderful expression!

3. Partner Reading: Repeated Reading (Checkout Opportunity)

While students do Partner Reading, listen to individuals read the passage. Work on accuracy and fluency, as needed.

4. Homework: Repeated Reading

Have students read the story at home.

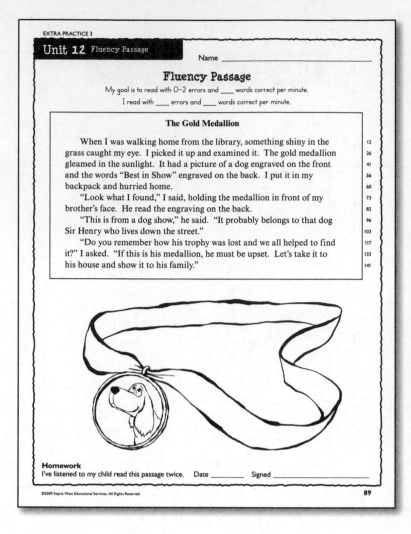

EXTRA PRACTICE 3

Unit 12 Fluency Passage

Name _____

Fluency Passage

My goal is to read with 0–2 errors and ____ words correct per minute.

I read with ____ errors and ____ words correct per minute.

The Gold Medallion

When I was walking home from the library, something shiny in the   12
grass caught my eye. I picked it up and examined it. The gold medallion   26
gleamed in the sunlight. It had a picture of a dog engraved on the front   41
and the words "Best in Show" engraved on the back. I put it in my   56
backpack and hurried home.   60

"Look what I found," I said, holding the medallion in front of my   73
brother's face. He read the engraving on the back.   82

"This is from a dog show," he said. "It probably belongs to that dog   96
Sir Henry who lives down the street."   103

"Do you remember how his trophy was lost and we all helped to find   117
it?" I asked. "If this is his medallion, he must be upset. Let's take it to   133
his house and show it to his family."   141

Homework
I've listened to my child read this passage twice.   Date _____   Signed _____

89

PROCEDURES

For each step, demonstrate and guide practice, as needed. Then have students complete the page independently.

1. Activity
Passage Comprehension

- Have students read each sentence or question, then fill in the bubble and/or blank with the correct answer.
- Think aloud with students and discuss the multiple-choice options, as needed.

Paragraph Comprehension

- Have students read the paragraph.
- Have students read each numbered sentence, then fill in the blank.
- Have students read the completed sentences.

Self-monitoring

Have students read and check their work, then draw a happy face in the Check and Correct circle.

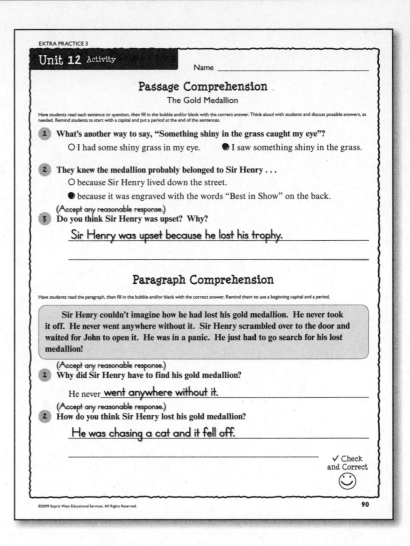

EXTRA PRACTICE 3

Unit 12 Activity

Name _____

Passage Comprehension
The Gold Medallion

Have students read each sentence or question, then fill in the bubble and/or blank with the correct answer. Think aloud with students and discuss possible answers, as needed. Remind students to start with a capital and put a period at the end of the sentences.

1 What's another way to say, "Something shiny in the grass caught my eye"?
○ I had some shiny grass in my eye.   ● I saw something shiny in the grass.

2 They knew the medallion probably belonged to Sir Henry . . .
○ because Sir Henry lived down the street.
● because it was engraved with the words "Best in Show" on the back.

(Accept any reasonable response.)
3 Do you think Sir Henry was upset? Why?
Sir Henry was upset because he lost his trophy.

Paragraph Comprehension

Have students read the paragraph, then fill in the bubble and/or blank with the correct answer. Remind them to use a beginning capital and a period.

Sir Henry couldn't imagine how he had lost his gold medallion. He never took it off. He never went anywhere without it. Sir Henry scrambled over to the door and waited for John to open it. He was in a panic. He just had to go search for his lost medallion!

(Accept any reasonable response.)
1 Why did Sir Henry have to find his gold medallion?
He never went anywhere without it.

(Accept any reasonable response.)
2 How do you think Sir Henry lost his gold medallion?
He was chasing a cat and it fell off.

✓ Check and Correct

©2009 Sopris West Educational Services. All Rights Reserved.   90

2. Word Fluency (BLMs are located on the CD.)

You may wish to have students repeat practice with Extra Practice, Word Fluency A or B.